Jobs, Heroes, Zeroes and Thieves!

By: Dennis "Ace" Reilly

To order additional copies of this book, contact:
Xlibris Corporation
1-888-795-4274
www.Xlibris.com
Orders@Xlibris.com
102156

This Book is based on Actual Events.

ACKNOWLEDGMENTS

Of the fifty-one jobs I've been employed in my 59 years of existence, the greatest of them all was being a firefighter for the New York City Fire Department. The vivid memories of commitment and self-sacrifice given by those who gave their all and perished on 9/11/2001 will never be forgotten. I want to thank them for the strength, courage, and desire they shared with those who worked with them. Unfortunately for the world, they are heroes who will no longer be heard from and enjoyed because of an evil human being and his followers. I want to thank our Navy Seals for imposing the justice Osama bin Laden so richly deserved upon him May 1 of 2011. Not a day goes by where I don't think about my 343 friends and colleagues.

With inspiration from my fallen friends, wife, the media and colleagues—I was able to vindicate myself after being abused and maligned by the Plantation, Florida Police Department. I continue to substantiate and investigate the family who robbed myself—and many others—of our life savings; including the five officers who escaped without discipline.

A special thanks goes out to Anne W. who gave fantastic advice to immortalize this book—and drove from Washington D.C. to our firehouse in N.Y.C. directly after 9/11/2001 to give us a huge stash of food and deliver a personal thank you. The individuals I associate with have tremendous work ethics and will do whatever it takes to make an honest living. There is never a job too demeaning—if that is what it takes to survive—and I must thank all of them for prompting me to deliver this message.

Last, but not least, I would like to thank the memory of my father. Brothers John, Ray, and Pat, and of course wife Cindy for their strength and support. Also for the countless hours Cindy contributed to the editing of this manuscript—and for dealing with a grouchy, old author.

"An honest and bright future awaits those who fight for self-determination by working hard and frowning upon handouts and cronyism."

Your Friend,

Dennis Reilly

INTRODUCTION

When I see all the unemployed people in our country and hear the politicians pontificating about how we need jobs—*like they're telling us something we don't know*—I think back to my working career. I know there are jobs out there; you just have to be committed and pursue them. If you really want a job, you can find one. I know this because I always have. If you can't find a job, then start your own business. No one says you have to like your job, but it's only fair to provide for yourself until you discover your niche.

I always searched for honest work. Any employment I secured, I strived to be the best at my position. At the age of five I wanted the best lemonade stand on the block, so I used fresh lemons and had infinite ice at the ready. Neighbors sought me out to mow lawns and shovel their walks because they knew my work would be exemplary. Honest effort and a *never-say-die* attitude is all that is warranted for successful employment. The following are employment positions I have held during my 59 years of existence:

1. Lemonade stand with fresh lemons

2. Lawn Mower Deluxe for my neighborhood

3. Bottle Collector—a .05¢ deposit was nice for the piggy bank

4. Paper Recycler—this is 1959 we're talking about. I'm way ahead of Gore.

5. Dog Walker of all sizes and breeds

6. Hospital Orderly

7. Grocery Store Shelf Stocker

8. Day Camp Laborer

9. Resident Assistant for college dormitory

10. Vacuum Cleaner Salesman

11. Night Watchman

12. Waiter and Dishwasher for Allied Medical Personnel, Inc.

13. Basketball Referee for high school and grade school

14. Crowd Controller for sporting events

15. Parks & Recreation Worker

16. Tennis Coach

17. Assistant Football Coach for my college

18. Dorm Director

19. Cement Loader and Laborer

20. History Teacher

21. Substitute Teacher for juveniles and high school

22. Hay Hauler

23. Painter

24. Construction Worker

25. Professional Football Linebacker

26. Professional Boxer

27. Moving Company Laborer

28. Jersey Docks Container Loader

29. Prefect for juvenile delinquents

30. Above Ground Pool Installer

31. Bar Bouncer

32. Bartender

33. Bus Driver

34. Lifeguard

35. Actor and Model

36. Comedian

37. Male Dancer

38. Night Recreation Manager

39. Group Leader at summer away camp

40. Boxing Trainer and Coach

41. Liquor Store Cashier

42. Firefighter

43. Personal Trainer

44. Fitness Class Instructor

45. Continuing Education Credits Provider for ACE and AFAA

46. Gym Owner

47. Gym Sales Professional

48. International Presenter

49. Fire Safety Director—New York Palace Hotel

50. Hotel Security

51. (You have to read the book!)

If the position presented itself where I had to make a living from any of the above employment, I would have succeeded with all (but may have had to expand the lemonade stand into a restaurant!!). There are stories and adventures attached to all of the noteworthy positions. My life was never boring. You may find roadblocks along your way, but nothing is insurmountable. The toils in life are both serious and comedic, and I'm certain you'll enjoy this never-ending job history. I hope President Obama will read my book and realize I should be vetted for Jobs Czar. If they don't like my solutions, I will clean the White House for a week!

CHAPTER 1

Dad And My First Job

My dad made certain each of his six sons knew that working was a necessity for a productive life. "You can be all you can be" and "the sky's the limit" were fashionable slogans for the times as long as you were employed. Dad worked his butt off to provide for mom and the six of us. His leadership was set by his example and he would let you know if you were a slacker. A good smack with the back of his hand or the threat of a strapping made me shake in my hand-me-down shoes. After fighting for his country in World War II, my father joined the ranks of New York's Finest. Al Sharpton would not have approved since he and Bill Ayers labeled the police "Pigs." I was proud of the man who was keeping New York City safe, and have the deepest respect for the police—even after being abused by five members of the Plantation, Florida Police Department in 2007. I judge people by the content of their character and not the color of their skin, and these five men in uniform made mine crawl.

When I was five years old I opened a lemonade stand outside our three-bedroom home on Perry Avenue in Staten Island, New York. This provided spare change in the summer. I don't think the lemonade was all that great, but the neighbors took care of a young kid and made me feel like a budding businessman. Mowing lawns and collecting bottles contributed to my savings, as well as collecting papers and hauling them to the recycler in my dad's 1950 wagon. Happy Rosen (proprietor of the local candy store) would get upset at the endless stream of bottles I retrieved. The fact I was protecting the environment and making some money was of no concern to his large behind! The neighbor across the street had a large Siberian husky and would pay me a couple of bucks a week to walk him. "Teddy" was about my size at this age and it became *him walking me* many a night. Dad gave me an allowance if I really needed something, but for the most part he wanted me to be self-reliant. I don't know what the politicians were like in this day, but assume they couldn't be as greedy and self-serving as today.

My clothes were hand-me-downs from my two older brothers and nothing ever fit, but I would never become a Renaissance man—since my big dream was to be a professional athlete.

That's me with the white socks and pants up to my knees holding "Brownie" the family dog. On my sixteenth birthday, dad took me to get my working papers so I could begin paying for social security. My aunt was a hospital nun at St. Vincent's and secured me a job as a delivery person/orderly at the facility. The cart was as big as me and was piled high to where I had a difficult time maneuvering through the spacious hallways. I worked non-stop and was never accustomed to a break, nor did I expect one. Mom and dad told me I was lucky to have a job and to be thankful someone would hire me. I had to wear a shirt and tie while delivering medicinal stock, but what did I care since I was making a salary? After all, they were paying me, and not the other way around. Dad always reminded us we weren't entitled to anything. I'm sure I wasn't in a union because my lunch was one half hour and there were no breaks. *Why should there be?* The best part was that no union dues were subtracted from my earnings and I received a raise after six months.

I had to wait two weeks for my first check and was taken aback when my mom explained it was suppose to go to your father. "But I was the one who worked for it," I argued. She began screaming at me, so I presented it to dad when he came home from work. He could see I was kind of disappointed, but I accepted the fact my dad deserved the money for steering me in the right direction. He smiled and returned the check while praising me for the consideration. What a guy, I was one lucky kid! Not because he gave me the money, but because he was my father. There was only one bathroom for eight and three of us kids slept in one room, but it was great and I always considered myself blessed.

Poor dad had to haul all six of us around for baseball games, and this was the first sport I considered greatness for myself. I sold decals in my over-sized uniform and thought I looked fabulous, but as you can see from this photo (I'm the kid standing on the far left) I am the dork of dorks. My oldest brother John was coach and dad was the manager (pictured back and from the left). I can remember calling another manager by his last name one afternoon as we traveled to the park and dad reamed me out like never before. I still call my elders Mister to this day unless they say otherwise.

I was considered one of the better basketball players at my elementary school. What did I know? My parents enrolled us in a Catholic grade school called St. Rita's. I don't know how they managed bringing up six kids on the salary of a cop and part-time nurse. Mom served in the military, also, and both were Disciplinarian's. We think mom wanted a girl but had no luck, and abortion was taboo for Irish Catholics. Dad enjoyed watching us grow and dragging us around to sporting events, but mom couldn't handle the enormity of it all and would vacation for periods of time with poor dad stuck with six muckety-mucks. He thrived on adversity and was able to juggle the gaggle of us like a walk in the park. We might not have had the best clothes, but we weren't naked and never in need of nourishment. One day I told dad I wanted to be a professional basketball player. He warned me you have to be incredible to get there. I was kind of ticked off he didn't have confidence in me, but later realized he was preparing me for reality. As I found out, good at St. Rita's didn't mean diddly. In sixth grade I was introduced to pee-wee football by another classmate. Steve Lopez excitedly explained it was the greatest sport he ever played. I just had to join, and while mom was hesitant, dad let me apply. It was love at first sight. My sights were set on playing professional football.

CHAPTER 2

Keep Your Village

I remember Hillary Clinton's book, *It Takes A Village,* and wondered what she was implying. She is now Secretary of State and never lived in a village, and I pondered what she could mean by such a blanket statement. All I ever needed was a dad, and most individuals I am associated with feel similar. My beef is why Hillary thinks others need a village, but not her. This reinforced my opinion of her as an elitist. If your parents were good enough for you, ours are good enough for us. Don't insult my mom and dad while earning money scribing a manuscript that claims we need a village to succeed.

Just like I always told my students and clients, "If I can do it, anybody can." The same applies to you, Hillary. There is some luck when it comes to success, but in politics it takes a lot of boot licking and somebody else's money, to whom you sell your soul. I remember Hillary being vilified for making $100,000 on cattle futures. While I don't begrudge her getting the money, I always wondered why she didn't share her secret with the rest of the country so they could gain a similar windfall. Now that might take a village!

I began high school joining my two older brothers at Monsignor Farrell High. I went to football camp, which was a big deal in 1969—paid for by dad—and did well. When school classes began I was turned off by the strict rules of the Christian brothers. Heck, if you walked up the wrong stairway you received one-hour detention (stand in a square for sixty minutes after school). My mom permitted me to switch to public high without consulting dad, and he was furious at his middle son. He wouldn't speak to me for a day, completely ignored me, which was unlike him. Mom was agreeable because she saved on the tuition, but dad knew this would have helped my athletic career. He just threw away all that money on football camp, but picked me up at Port Richmond High School two days later and apologized to me. He was wise beyond his years and confided I could make it anywhere if I applied myself. I was the kid who was wrong, but my father let it slide and encouraged me to make it big with the public schools.

This is a far cry from the elites who occupy our political landscape wasting our tax dollars on a broken system where they refuse to send their children. Just look at the children of the surviving presidents and see where their kids went to school, if you doubt me.

Hillary wants us common folk *in a village* where she controls our habits and purse strings. After all, her and Bill know better (just ask Monica Lewinsky).

Dad let me concentrate on sports because he knew I wanted it. After retiring from the police department he went to work as a caretaker at the local Roman Catholic church. Holy Family recognized a great man when they hired John Reilly, and I would help him when time permitted while in high school and home from college. He worked there until coming down with lung cancer in 1976. I broke my collarbone one week before our first high school football game in 1970. I went to a local doctor and succeeded in deceiving him to make out a doctor's note giving me a clean bill of health. The doctor had no idea my collarbone was broken, but cleared me to play football under the assumption of a normal physical exam. Upon completion of the appointment I told the doctor my coach was concerned about a sore shoulder, and he scribbled that it was fine after examining the opposite one. When a doctor writes, it is nearly illegible; so when he scribbled *right shoulder* it looked like *left shoulder* and the note fooled Coach Bilotti.

Who would figure my dad would show up at a game I wouldn't be participating in? But he sensed my shenanigans and I went from ecstatic to terrified when our eyes locked after I recovered a fumble in the end zone. I played the entire fourth quarter contemplating my fate, and when the game ended he strode to greet me across the field. I remained silent and his first words were about how deceived the coach would feel if he knew I had put one over on him. I tried to cover and said I had seen a doctor, but dad knew the deal and just shook his head. He never said another word about it. He figured if the kid wants to put his health on the line for a dream he is seeking, so be it. It's better than being a lazy SOB expecting to have things handed to you. He taught me well because dad would have done the same.

During that summer I was helping dad at the church bingo hall unloading and setting up tables while boasting about my chest size and biceps. At this time I really didn't have a great physique and hadn't a clue what real training was all about. My dad looked at me admiring myself and said, "You're not in any kind of shape, you're soft!" I was shocked and ticked off like I'd never been, but couldn't muster a response. Upon finishing my senior year I joined a gym. I would show dad how soft I was!

A buddy of mine joined the "Y" with me and I secured jobs at a Waldbaum's supermarket and as a grounds worker at a Jewish day camp. My duties at Waldbaum's were to stock shelves and unload containers. At the camp my high school gym teacher/basketball coach boss had me chopping wood, catching ducks, varnishing picnic tables, and raking the stone parking lot. Off days I worked out twice a day and they were killers. I'll never be in that kind of shape again. It was my life. Lift for an hour and a half, run five miles, and then work out for another ninety minutes. Two other friends joined me and we would leave puddles on the floor we sweat so much. The competition was incredible. We were doing twenty chin-ups, thirty dips, 300 bench press, 250 press, a thousand sit-ups and leg raises besides all the body building exercises we threw into the mix.

I sat out the year after high school and worked a local construction job sweeping floors, delivering furniture, breaking concrete and anything else the boss needed accomplished. I did sets of twenty-five push-ups and run 40-yard wind sprints when time permitted. The pay was decent and it was forty hours a week. I had a car that I purchased from a neighbor for $300. It was a 1964 Corvair and my buddies named it the "green machine" because smoke came out of the vents when I drove it too long.

I remember running into some girls I knew from high school about six months after I began working out seriously and their mouths were agape as to how muscular I had become. They didn't say anything, but I could tell from their expressions they were shocked at the transformation. My friends had been telling me I was huge, but I never really thought about it since I only wanted to beat my buddies in the strength competitions. Dad never said anything one way or the other, but when I decided to go in the golden gloves that winter, he signed off over mom's objections. I was seventeen and a parental signature was required to fight.

I was a dumb kid and went down to a local gym to train for the gloves. The trainer's name was Ray Rivera. After me (the local football hero) and Nick Fotiu (the local hockey star) beat each other around the ring, Ray explained he'd love to train us, but we needed another year of seasoning. Nick went on to play for the Rangers and I would get my shot with the Giants, but I decided to fight that year anyhow since I was accepted into Missouri Valley College and would play football in the fall.

I trained myself at the local "Y" and would spar occasionally with a middleweight friend named Dean Fiorella. His brother was in the gloves the previous year and his trainer would act as our second. I soon learned why we needed another year. I won my first bout against an opponent who was fat and out of shape. My brother Jim questioned if I found him in the bowery and asked him to participate, but I had achieved new-found fame and my photo was featured on the front page of the Daily News delivering a left hand to the face of Rodriguez. The second fight at Madison Square Garden did not go as well. C.J. Brown was a seasoned fighter and had me outclassed. I never backed down although I was dropped after I pummeled Brown on the ropes. My grandmother was at ringside begging me to get up, and I finished the bout chasing after the elusive but effective Brown. With even minimal experience I could have dropped this guy, and now I know why Ray Rivera insisted I wait.

After the disappointment I went back to my training in earnest, figuring college would be more intense than high school. And our our high school coach just about killed us!

CHAPTER 3

Missouri Is Hot

Our high school team stunk and Coach Gibler only offered me a scholarship if I proved myself. It was 105 degrees when I exited the plane in Kansas City. Marshall is one hour from the airport and the college sent a van to pick me up. This was my first time on a plane. I never had the opportunity or money to fly. Unlike Nancy Pelosi, I couldn't travel first class and bill it to the taxpayer. The landscape was barren and it became hotter as we neared the campus. Missouri Valley is Division II and I learned training camp was paid for by work done by the freshmen (me). I needed rest, but instead had to paint fences and cut grass between workouts in the scorching midday sun.

The practices weren't near as difficult as high school. The man-makers at seven in the morning were arduous, but only lasted about fifteen minutes. Scrimmaging and drills were similar to high school, but a lot more technical. Sprints after the practice session consisted of four 40-yard dashes; a far cry from the fifty we were required to do in high school. I remember the time one kid went down in high school while we sprinted and coach screamed for us to run over him rather than help him to his feet. The comparison of high school and college practice was incredulous. I trained my butt off figuring it would be more demanding than high school physically, but was pleasantly surprised. The coach wanted you in shape, but he didn't allow you to leave it on the field. To run just to run is counter-productive, and I learned the hard way.

Being a freshman is no bargain, and the heat and obscurity had me thinking about enlisting in the service. My lottery number was 200, and the year prior the draft reached 220, so I figured I'd be a shoo-in. This was during the height of the Vietnam War and protests were rampant on the college campuses. My brother Jimmy visited school on his way to an army base in Kansas and wasn't enamored with my plans to enlist. He urged me to concentrate on football and said if I were drafted, it would be for two years rather than the four if you enlist. I took his advice. The following year the number only hit 90 before the war was shut down completely. My football career blossomed.

I became a resident assistant in my dormitory, thanks to the football coach lobbying for me. It was a great job because you had to look out for the residents on your floor and they were all friends anyhow. I found work as a waiter in a local restaurant, and Cecil (the boss) was a nice enough guy, but ruled with an iron hand. He fired the cook for squeezing the juice out of the hamburgers, so I decided to boycott the unfair layoff and was let go myself. There was no Jesse Jackson to stick up for us and blackmail the company with unruly demonstrations, so I found employment as a vacuum cleaner salesman. The vacuums were revolutionary 1973 and used water to clean, but I wasn't able to sell any and the owner cheated me out of the base salary he promised. Again, no Al Sharpton to come to my rescue, but I survived and was hired by a security firm named "Guardsmark" for Banquet Foods.

The factory ran six blocks long and I was assigned the graveyard shift. My boss was a Korean war veteran named Sgt. Hammer. Cecil Ardsley and Thaddeus Gilmore were the other two elderly guards. I was issued a square badge and standard security uniform. My only weapon was a night-stick and I carried a time clock to punch in at the different stations. Each night I was required to fill out a report, and things were so uneventful I made up stories about Gilmore and Ardsley giving me obscene gestures, setting booby traps and trying to mow me down in a van. The more outrageous the story, the more the sergeant laughed. After reading my tales he would cross my writings out and provide his own version of reality.

I found myself almost falling asleep in some classes, but managed to fight through the fatigue. Hell, my brother John had signed up for his second tour in Vietnam to give me a shot at playing the sport I loved, so what right did I have to complain? Unlike high school when I was satisfied with mediocre grades, I strove to be the best I could be in college and made Dean's List. President Obama might say Missouri Valley College can't hold a candle to his beloved Harvard, but I'll put my college football coach (Ken Gibler) up against anyone in the world as a mentor and scholar. He always prayed before a game that God would give us the strength, courage, and desire to do the best job we are capable of doing. When I see politicians patting themselves on the back and eulogizing one another as to how great they are, and were, I think of my father and Coach Gibler. With their knowledge and courage, these political frauds couldn't compare to them.

I decided I could make some pocket money officiating high school basketball games and gave that a whirl. You had to keep on your toes and deal with the wrath of the spectators, but it prepared me to cope with other opportunities that would present themselves. Officials had to keep in shape, or you would look like a slug if the high-schoolers beat you up and down the floor. Getting paid while keeping in shape was the kind of job I dreamed about daily. Only in my fantasy I'm wearing a New York Giants football uniform. *Make that ANY professional football uniform!*

Local high schools would sometimes hire me to control the crowd, collect fees and guard the cash box at big games. I didn't have a gun, so I guess they thought my presence was a deterrent. Forty bucks for watching an exciting athletic contest was fine by me.

CHAPTER 4

Senior Summer

I was about 6'1" and 220 pounds coming into my senior year. That summer my buddy got me a job as a recreation counselor with the New York City Parks Department. He informed me I would have to join the Democratic political party to get the position. I joined, but really didn't care much about politics and never questioned why I was forced to become a Democrat. My friend told me to see some Ph.D. in political science at the party headquarters, and a week later I was told to report for my position. Not realizing it at the time, I was pushed ahead of someone because I had a connection, and the woman in charge of the bureau of parks let me know about it. She reamed me out, and I was about to tell the old bag to shove the job where the sun doesn't shine, but she softened up and assured me the employment was mine. I contemplated why she eased up, and figured my contact was her boss *and she did not want to be demoted!* I felt bad about the situation, and eased my guilt by reasoning she had the job ready for one of her cronies.

The park to which I was assigned was out in the boondocks and nobody ever showed up to play. It was the most deserted playground I ever witnessed; myself and two other recreation specialists never had to do anything in the way of recreation. No one showed to play basketball or take advantage of our expertise in fitness. A boss would show his face towards the end of the day and collect the time sheets. Talk about a waste of taxpayer dollars. This was my introduction to the government largesse that has multiplied exponentially since 1974.

I spiked my workouts for the upcoming season and did sprints, push-ups and chins at the park while on city time. There was never any interruption and I had the grass and trees all to myself. My co-workers went to the beach most of the time and I would sign them out in the evening, if the boss came around, or they would do it themselves in the morning. Accountability in government is non-existent and it seeps down to those in the trenches because the leaders at the top are rich, power hungry and lazy. I made a note to never work for the government unless I could endure a life with no challenges and self-discipline.

My gym workouts were incredible. A weight lifting fanatic introduced me to a small blue pill called Dianabol, or D-bol, and it caused my strength and stamina to skyrocket. Where I was doing a 350-pound bench press for one repetition, I was now completing sets of ten with the same weight. I was throwing around 250 with the overhead press and squatting with four hundred pounds for reps. My speed was increasing and the steroid enabled me to work harder and faster. It cut down on your recovery time, but if you didn't put in the time and effort, the supplement was for naught.

I told my aunt, Sister Regina Helen, about my new elixir and she began sending me articles on the serious side effects. By this time, I was beginning training camp in Missouri and my digestive system was giving me problems. I ditched the pill after two months of use and returned to normal. I was able to keep most of my gains through hard work and a healthy diet, but the magic pill gives you a boost if you hit the wall in your progressions. These substances are now banned because they *do* offer an advantage for those who take them. It is not a magic pill, however, and I had to work even harder for the two months I used it in 1974.

My senior year of college was fantastic for a kid who came from a high school team that had a 3-and-5 record with lopsided losses in our first and last games. We ended up number two in the nation and were undefeated until the championship game. I was voted most valuable player; N.A.I.A. Division II All American; most valuable defensive back; MVP in the college homecoming game; and I was runner-up in the Kansas City Golden Gloves Heavyweight Division. The only negative was I separated my shoulder the last regular season game and played the semi-finals and championship game at a severe disadvantage. This caused more damage to my shoulder, so I rehabbed the following year while working as a graduate assistant football coach at Missouri Valley College, head tennis coach at Missouri Valley, dorm director for Moreland Hall, and a substitute teacher at Marshall High School.

That summer I worked at U.S. Gypsum Corp. on Staten Island where I loaded pallets with fifty-pound cement bags. I broke the record for poundage produced in a day and my supervisor loved me. The union workers made me cease for a lunch break the day I achieved the milestone, and I couldn't understand why they didn't want me to succeed. My face and body was covered with cement by the finish of my eight-hour shift, and my boss said anytime I was seeking work, he would have it for me.

I lived on top of a neighborhood bar that summer for $120 per week, where I was required to habitate in a small room and had to share the bath. The walls were paper-thin, and I could hear all the sexual excitement from the rum-balls coming in at five in the morning. If I worked the night shift, I would sometimes get a 10AM wake up from a drunk who couldn't find his room. Don't ever live on top of a bar with a bathroom you have to share!

CHAPTER 5

I Like Coaching

How lucky could a guy be? I was working for a man I played for and admired. We had a lot of talent, and another buddy (Gary Maher—offensive tackle) was working as a graduate assistant alongside me. For a guy who was always shy with the women, I was coming into my own and had more girlfriends than I thought possible. I finally had my own home (dorm director apartment) where I thought I would reside for at least a year. The salary wasn't great, but I was learning the art of coaching; utilities were free, and I had a satisfactory workout facility at my disposure.

There were drawbacks, since some of my buddies would take advantage of me being the coach. One kid wanted me to list him at six feet so he might have a shot at the professionals. Did he not think they might check his height if he made it that far? And if you look 5'10", proclaiming you are taller won't be of much assistance. The same fellow and another friend would slack in the workouts when performing with my group. I encouraged them to work harder, not for me but for the team, and it fell on deaf ears. Like Coach Gibler said on so many occasions, "The cream always rises to the top."

I enjoyed inspiring others through my own actions and expected the same effort from those I coached. My mindset would not permit me to be a slacker. When I overheard the "Big Tackle" (he was 6'5" and 260, but soft) telling anyone who would listen he was going to lift weights and run all summer and come back like a Greek God, I lit into him. "There are two months left until summer recess, so start right now with your program. What are you waiting for?!!!" He didn't heed my advice, and the following year he came back even flabbier—with a girl on his arm and a cigarette in his mouth. He decided football was too much for him and quit the team.

An unfortunate aspect of being graduate assistant is you have to scout the opposing team for the following week's game, which meant long van rides and missing your own team in action. You have to start at the bottom up, and scouting is an important part of coaching that doesn't get recognized except to those on the team who take the game seriously. Speed and strength is important, but smarts separate the great from the very good. Attitude plays a role, and malcontents can be a drag on an entire program. It is best to weed them out, and most often they will do it themselves. You learn as you live, and I was certain the team names might change for me in the future, but the characters would remain the same.

I went to a St. Louis Cardinal open tryout that spring and received a letter a few weeks later asking me to come to summer camp. My forty-yard dash time was 4.7 seconds, which was about average for an N.F.L. linebacker in 1975. They didn't ask me back after the mini-camp, and the head coach of Moberly High School in Moberly, Missouri (he was a senior when I was a freshman at Missouri Valley) asked me to be his defensive coach and a History instructor at the school. History was my minor and I accepted the offer.

That summer I remained in Missouri, rented a trailer home, and hauled hay. I used my hands as meat hooks; and the work was hard, but bearable. This is not a job I would recommend for a politician, since they would actually have to sweat for a living. Just throwing bales of hay on a tractor all day in 100-degree heat is beneath the academics who believe they rule us peons.

I put out a feeler with the Giants, since a coach from one of the schools we played in Kansas (Ottawa U) knew their personnel director. Besides hauling hay, I painted buildings and smashed concrete that summer in Moberly—together with doing my football workouts.

My trailer-home rental was furnished and the mattress was two-inch-thick foam. It was fine for a guy who didn't know how the politicians lived, but I was upset when crickets infested the place through some unknown vent pipes. I had to fog them out; and for a fortnight I had nightmares of Jiminy-Cricket from the Disney Show.

The team was coming off a one-and-nine season and there was a lot of work to accomplish. A winning attitude had to be established, and I worked out with the team in their fledgling weight room. The kids were enthusiastic and showed potential—and appreciated the fact I went through their summer paces with them. I incorporated much of what Coach Gibler taught me and always added my own flavor to the mix. I considered myself a disciplinarian, but was not near as rigid as my high school coach. Respect is something you earn, and I made certain to treat everyone equally and demonstrated that I wouldn't ask anyone to do anything I wouldn't do myself.

The social studies department chairwoman (my boss) was a stickler for detail, and I attacked my curriculum with fervor. I loved our founding fathers and enjoyed teaching American History, World Geography, Civics and Social Events. The lesson plans were changed depending on my mood, since I didn't want to keep repeating the same outlines year after year. That is what I consider being lazy and an injustice to the kids you are being paid to educate. One of my footballers stopped me after class one afternoon and explained how he hated History until he took my class.

It was the fact I made the characters come to life, was what he enjoyed so much. The satisfaction was almost as good as winning the big game. In fact, I think I felt better because he made me realize no one wants a boring teacher who just reads from the text.

Being in front of a class was no problem, since the department chairman who I did my student teaching under at Marshall High School handed me the attendance book my first day and said the class is yours. What a deal! He got paid to have me teach his class while he read the paper and had breakfast. I had to learn on my feet, but the students were courteous and Coach Naylor gave me the highest grade you could receive.

I knew I would miss playing, but watching the kids progress and applying what you taught them was satisfying indeed. When I was in high school I would've run through a brick wall for the coach; no questions asked! Maybe it was just me, but I noticed a little less of that at Moberly. It was most likely just me being overly optimistic because I always had such respect for authority. Times were slowly changing, but these students were fantastic compared to what I would encounter in the future.

We ended up with a five-and-three record, and I know I was hard on some of the guys, but could tell they appreciated the effort I put into my job. You were a coach, father, friend and confidant to a bunch of kids not all that younger than you. Our spring training session began soon after the season ended, and for me it never stopped. You keep working hard and you don't have to worry about getting out of shape. Just laying around for months is not a lifestyle conducive to being the best you can be. Anytime someone claims to work hard and put in extraordinary hours exercising, take a look at their body. If they are soft, you know it's a bunch of mush they're talking. The best example I can give is the politician. I needn't say more!

I was ecstatic! It was like waking up as a kid on Christmas morning. Our family didn't have much, but my parents genuinely overdid it for us kids on Christ's birthday. A letter arrived at my humble trailer home with the logo of the New York Giants stamped impressively on the facade. The personnel director was inviting me to training camp and informed me I received rave reviews from a coach he knew in Kansas. He asked me to contact him, which I did immediately, and he informed me as to when I would report. Camp would be held at Pace University in Pleasantville, New York, and I would sign my contract on arrival.

John Morris (my buddy at Missouri Valley and the head coach who hired me to coach at Moberly) asked me to take a leave of absence rather than resign, but I replied there was no way I wasn't going to succeed, and I voided my contract mid year so that I could go home and concentrate on getting ready. It was sad leaving the young adults I had been working with in the classroom and on the field, and the hundreds of personal farewell notes made me feel both happy and guilty. My departure was quick and I asked John to forward me all my trophies, yearbooks and personal items I could not fit in my loaded car. To this day, I have not received my prized possessions. John disappeared and was divorced, last I heard, and I'm sure my hardware and memories are in the trash somewhere in Missouri.

I found a job with Bekins [moving company] when I arrived in New York City and bought a car for two hundred bucks that was nothing to look at and left a trail of smoke in it's wake. My youngest brother was a gifted mechanic and he fixed it up as best he could. The upholstery and seats were worn through and through; and this machine was not conducive for dating.

My indestructible father came down with lung cancer and had to have one lung removed. He did fine for a few months and never complained while my mom harassed him continuously. John Reilly was a saint and I never heard him gripe my entire life . . . and we were always screwing up! My mom was never able to handle the rigors and inconvenience of having six boys (she wanted a girl and birth control was taboo for Catholics back then) and would leave home for weeks at a time while we grew up. It never fazed dad. He thrived in the environment—while I would have jumped off a bridge!! (if faced with his problems and workload)

Moving people was strenuous work and I teamed up with a guy named Pete Pullara (who would later play for the Browns). We would try to outdo the other and haul wardrobes up spiral staircases without thinking about it. He was a defensive tackle and put me to shame most of the time. I remember working our tails off for some bigwig moving into a penthouse in midtown Manhattan and the guy stiffed us because we left a half-inch scrape carrying a piano up a difficult stairway. We wanted to crack him, but thought better of it. He didn't even say thank you because we were peons to him. *Like the people are insignificant to the politicians.*

My training was going well and I devised personal drills for the skills I would need to make the team. I had no illusions of being the best, but sincerely believed I could stick. Special teams play was something I always excelled at, and my plan was to make the team through reckless abandon and learn and work my way up as a linebacker. The Giants had the best linebackers in the N.F.L. Carson, Kelley, Schmidt, Lloyd, Selfidge and VanPelt were proven entities around the league.

My dad was now in the hospital because the cancer returned; mom ordered me to leave the family home. I rented a small apartment and borrowed a friend's Camaro to drive to camp. If they saw the vehicle I called my own, Giant officials would think me a vagrant and have the car towed. Double sessions in the N.F.L. are brutal, more so when you are a free agent rookie out of a small school. You absolutely have to excel because they have nothing invested in you, while even the latest draft pick gets a small bonus. My contract was for the minimum, and I had to chuckle when I signed because there was nothing to negotiate. Heck, they could have offered me two grand and I would have accepted. It's funny because you sign for the $18,000 minimum at the time, but they have all these incentives—such as, making the pro ball and leading the team in interceptions—that bump it up to about fifty.

I was the smallest linebacker at 6' 220 lbs. My speed was between 4.7 and 4.8 for 40 yards, which was average for linebackers in the league at this time. John McVay was the head coach and only lasted the year. My tenure was less, only two exhibition games. What a disappointment! My dad was dying of cancer and his son was bounced from his lifetime dream. By the time I was let go, I weighed 201 pounds. I felt like a midget. I did get to tackle Larry Csonka in scrimmages, since he finished his career with the Giants. When I was a kid I always dreamed about signing autographs. Even during double sessions, kids would be bussed in to watch the practices. Guys like Csonka and Carson would drive their cars from the dorm to the field and skip out before the rush of screaming children seeking autographs. I would shower-up and hurry to the dorm to get much required rest before the next session, but the young swarms would stop you and ask for signatures. Wanting to hurry, I would explain I might not make the team, hoping they would leave me alone. Instead, they demanded my autograph while saying, "You might be good." *It didn't take away the stress and the aches, but it was comical.*

When I was told to bring my playbook to the general manager's office, I knew I was a goner. He offered me some contacts he had with the Canadian football league, but I declined. I was concerned about my dad and went to visit him in the hospital. His weight was down to sixty pounds and I could ascertain he was in extreme pain. I felt horrible and began to tell him I had been let go, and he pointed to the newspaper where it was spelled out in black and white. Dad was always a step ahead of everyone. With tubes injected throughout his body and barely able to speak, he told me to become a coach. He was my coach and mentor and wanted me to help others the way he did all of us. Dad passed on not long after and never complained about his situation. I moan about everything, but he took life the way it came at him. Just keep working and good things will happen. He is in heaven, no doubt!

CHAPTER 6

A Prefect for Juveniles

The apartment I had been living in was a horror. So I found a job in Lincolndale, New York working at a juvenile delinquent facility run by the Christian brothers. I could live there in the cottage with the residents and pay no rent or utilities. You were required to live there for your shifts anyhow. My two older brothers lived in Mamaroneck and Yonkers, which wasn't that far away, and I could stay with them on my off days. I was broke and needed to put some money away. My salary was $9,000 a year, and I would get paid as a substitute teacher for the kids at $30 per day, if I so chose.

The transmission went on the clunker I owned and I was forced to buy a car from a used-car dealer. My choice was a 1970 black Ford Maverick bought and paid for with my first $500 check. Of course, there were problems the sales guy conveniently refused to disclose, but my brother took care of them for me so I didn't have to throw a brick through the Lil Motors' (name of dealership) front window.

Lincolndale kids were troubled and street smart. All of them knew how to game the system. Most of them were transfers from the juvenile detention facility named Spofford on Rikers Island. Pickpockets, car thieves, violent assaults, rape, robbery, and a few murders were all included in their repertoire of crimes. Remember, they are all sixteen and under. The cottage held twenty-five juveniles of which you were constantly responsible. Their bunks were barracks-style with two private rooms for the head prefect and his assistant.

It would remind you of a college campus and consisted of a large dining hall, a school, athletic complex with a 440 all-weather track, three baseball diamonds, spacious gymnasium, infirmary, outdoor pool, meeting rooms, a theater, and a lock-up facility. The only gang was the Muslim five-percenters.

The food wasn't the greatest, but more than adequate. None of the Muslims would eat the ham and they called it swine. There were some good athletes and we conducted basketball and baseball leagues. The cottages competed against each other. I decided to box in the Golden Gloves that year and would use the cottage van to load some of the kids in with me to watch me spar. A strong 16-year-old middleweight named Gino bragged about his boxing ability, so I let him spar and he did well. He was a bully and picked on the others in the cottage. After whipping one of the skinny kids with a belt I remanded him to lock-up. The psychologists said he would not be put back in the general population, but Gino informed me that wouldn't last long. Less than a week later he was allowed back with the population and picked a fight with me while I was teaching a class. The brothers broke it up and Gino laughed about how they all get over on the liberal psychologists; and he was right. Before I left to go work for more money on the New Jersey docks, Gino told me he appreciated that I tried to help him, but he was beyond reach and would one day be in jail for murder. I pray it didn't work out that way.

There were so many hilarious incidents I had competing with the kids while trying to demonstrate a proper work ethic and attitude. One kid escaped on me when I took them to watch me spar in the Bronx, so he ruined it for the rest of us. I was working the night of the blackout and could smell the pot wafting throughout the cottage, but I was unable to find the culprits who had a fantastic adventure on how to get over on yours truly that evening. They loved playing poker and I would always win turkey and cheese sandwiches from the kid who escaped on me. Teaching gym class was as wild as it gets, since you had over fifty juveniles running around with basketballs attempting to wreak havoc on the one man in command. Anyone can show off a sheepskin and give a speech, but not everyone can survive in the trenches.

CHAPTER 7

Loading Trucks

A buddy of mine was a boss on the docks over in Port Newark, so he got me a job loading containers at the terminal. The pay was triple what I was making at Lincoln Hall and I was back in my hometown. I rented a room after spending a night in a sleazy hotel infested with bed-bugs. I had to share the bath, but I showered daily at the YMCA where I did my workouts.

I love physical work and that's really all this was. The container was backed into the port and you filled it with the items being shipped. Another college buddy was working with me and we would have a blast making up tales about the other workers to pass the time. What a motley crew this was with me included. Stanley was our heavyset, err, I mean fat boss who directed us with his manifest.

The warehouse was the size of an airport terminal, so employees on Hi-Los would transport the pallets to us loaders up front. It was summer and the blistering heat made me want to work harder. Once you get the blood flowing, it's all downhill. The good thing about this job was the variety of characters in a work force that included a few boozers, a couple of athletes, some hippies, and those looking to get by.

To relieve the monotony Brian (my college buddy) and I would plant stories pitting one worker against another. By the end of a week, people that never spoke to one another were at war. Irate employees were writing notes about each other and driving transporters into one another. I learned you can say outrageous canards to some individuals and they will perceive it as the gospel truth. One Napoleonic loader refused to work on the same platform with a large hippie dude. The dumbfounded supervisor was incredulous there could be complications about uplifting items into a container. The seeds of dissent are easily planted, but difficult to remedy. It was a comedy and it passed the time as to what otherwise would have been boring, but demanding employment.

On weekends I decided to make extra cash installing above-the-ground pools. I hadn't a clue how to accomplish this, but saw an ad in the *Advance* employment section and applied at Staten Island Pools. There were six crews of four. Two were bosses and the others diggers. Of course, I was a laborer or whatever you might want to call me. All the bosses did was use a level and figure out the dimensions where the pool would sit properly. The pools were circular and could be assembled within a few hours if all pitched in. It was summer and some guys didn't like to sweat for a living. I would learn to call them slackers, and us laborers needed to stand up for each other.

One stifling hot morning the 'boss guys' drove me and another worker to a site they hadn't completed the previous day. There was at least a day's worth of hard labor staring us in the face. They decided to drop me off to finish the digging by my lonesome. The other laborer refused to leave me stranded and told the boss slackers there was no way I could handle this myself. They permitted him to stay with me—and we likened ourselves to Papillon being interned at the prison camp in French Guiana: "Welcome to the penal colony of French Guiana, whose prisoners you are, and from which there is no escape." We laughed all day at our plight while our hands blistered and muscles cramped, but we finished and clocked out with two hours overtime to boot!

CHAPTER 8

Return To Coaching

I took a pay cut to coach at my high school with a former teammate (who had been working there since graduating) and with our inaugural mentor, Nick Guts Bilotti. Nick also secured me employment as a physical education teacher/bodyguard for the principal. I was only paid $40 per diem, which had been lowered from $120.00 because of the budget crunch. The money I was allotted for coaching was a meager $200.00 from the father's club for a year-round job where you were a father figure, trainer, counselor, and football technician for teenagers.

To make ends meet, I had to work security at a bar called Doherty's on Wednesdays and weekends where you were assured of a few weekly brawls with the local losers. They were insurmountable dirt bags who were smelly, sloppy and soused on alcohol attempting to pick up babes who wanted nothing to do with them; which, in turn, angered them to a fit of rage. I kicked one such loser's behind on a particular evening and he ended up becoming a chief in the fire department! *Can civil service exams be so difficult, Al Sharpton, if this guy could become chief?*

The attitude of the youth changed dramatically since I was in high school, all of six years earlier. Where I never talked back to a coach other than to say, "Yes, sir," no matter what I might think of his remarks, these players had a new outlook on authority. I remember asking one of my better linebackers why he was late for practice and he answered I was lucky he showed up. Six years ago Guts Bilotti would have kicked me in the butt for making the same comment, but now was afraid of a lawsuit. Thank you, ACLU, for helping our youth become such mature, disciplined adults!

Some of the players (while decent talent-wise for high school, but lacking for intelligence in the classroom) asked me to get them tryouts with the Giants because they would "never make it in college." They were shocked when I explained they weren't good enough and that you needed to be smart on the gridiron. A few even asked me if they should take steroids—when they didn't know the foggiest about working out! In their shallow minds, these young men surmised you swallowed a pill and became big, strong and fast.

I was broke, without a bank account, and the apartment I rented by the school was so rat-infested I thought I might be eaten alive on my mattress floor bed. With my deposit already secured, the proprietor acted surprised by my confirmation of rats on the premises and refused to refund my security, even when I moved into one of his room rentals in the vicinity. Fortunately, the derelicts with whom I now shared the kitchen and bath verified there were no vermin on site. I moved out in less than a month because I got the hives and my food kept getting pilfered from the community refrigerator. Room walls were paper-thin and I could hear animations of sexual prowess constantly for the second time in my life.

One Friday morning on my return from employment at the bar I noticed our starting running back cavorting with a female outside a cocktail lounge in a state of inebriation. This was the morning of a game, so I relayed this to the head coach and he suspended the kid for the contest—while letting it be known I was the informant! The team members were furious with me, as was the suspended player. I was happy he was upset about not playing, but informed him he let the team down by not preparing himself properly for the game. How he could expect to perform to the best of his ability was a discipline he was never confronted with. His dad later thanked me for my concern, but I was upset with the head guy for putting the blame on his assistant.

My assignment was to coach the defensive backs and linebackers. One of the backers had a politically connected dad, but lacked the hard-nosed attitude you require to be a standout. If I had my way he wouldn't have been starting, but the head coach saw it differently and the kid ended up making the all-star team. This was my second brush with politics. And the smell was sickening.

At our last game of the season, I was in the press box sending down plays and formations I thought we could run effectively. None of them were being utilized and we were getting our butts kicked. Monsignor Farrell (opposing team) didn't need to pass because they were gaining

8-10 yards a clip. I didn't need the headphones because I was screaming to go into goal line in the middle of the field. We had to stop the run before we needed to worry about the pass. My recommendations fell on deaf ears and I knew it was time to coach elsewhere and begin to earn some money.

CHAPTER 9

The Night Center

While teaching at Tottenville High School on Staten Island, I was hired to direct the school night center for students and adults. All I had to do was hang out for four hours and make certain the facility ran smoothly. Throwing out the basketballs and assisting in the weight room kept me busy, and it was fun when this is the career you have chosen. The pay could have been better than the $10.00 an hour I received, but I wasn't complaining. Some nights I would work out with the members if numbers were light. The equipment could have been more updated. The speed bag the city supplied was the size of a balloon and some of the basketballs were of the Naismith era, but we made do.

CHAPTER 10

Camp Olympus

A physical education colleague at Port Richmond High School was part owner of an overnight camp located in the Catskill Mountain area. He petitioned me to work as a group director for fifty children and four counselors summer of 1979. For two months duration the pay wasn't much, but I figured I'd be helping the young adults with fitness and life, so I readily agreed. The department chairman (my high school football coach) advised me against it, but I could use the extra money and would be receiving free meals to go with my meager pay. If coach had offered me some kind of summer work, I may have heeded his warning.

The drive to Camp Olympus took me three hours and the grounds were both spacious and beautiful. My colleague (Chuck Schwartz) and his wife had their own spacious quarters; and his partner was a year-round resident who lived in a beautiful, expansive house on the premises. As I arrived, Chuck motioned me to keep driving up the road to my quarters with the assistant director. I pulled my vehicle into a small space and saw the buses unloading kids in front of five medium-sized barracks.

After exiting my 1960 Ford Maverick, I asked the assistant where my quarters were. He pointed to one of the barracks in which the counselors were directing the kids. He could tell from the stunned look on my face

I wasn't happy as I followed him into the staff office. The phone rang immediately and I overheard Chuck asking him about my reaction. His reply was that I seemed stunned. I said nothing and walked to my summer home thinking maybe I could deal with it.

To my astonishment, I learned I would be in a bunk the size of a child's sporting a two-inch sponge mattress and have absolutely no privacy. I would be sharing the toilets and bathroom facilities with kids and counselors, forcing me to bend down to shower. I stormed into the assistant director's office and told him to ring Chuck. I told him this was a no-go, but he pleaded for me to try it for an evening. One night was enough. My feet hung a foot over the bed, my butt barely fit on the toilet, there was no heat or hot water, and a constant noise emanated in the bunks.

After a sleepless eight hours, I heard revelry at 6AM and saw Chuck standing bare-chested in the middle of the five barracks, looking refreshed and eager to go after a good night's sleep. I told him I was leaving if he didn't get me private accommodations, and he acceded, putting me up in a room at his partner's mansion. I lasted three weeks before I had a falling out with his partner about inviting a female guest to my room. It was rewarding working and interacting with the kids, but I wasn't going to be pushed around by a guy I was doing a favor for. It was his loss and he knew it because everyone wanted me to remain; but the boss blew it, his apology was too late. I went home to the bar job.

That summer I secured gym memberships at a significant discount for the interested high school players and worked them out during my free time. I needed more money because my only employment was working at a local bar and Dangerfield's Night Club in Manhattan. Rodney Dangerfield claimed not to receive any respect. And he didn't disappoint me with the wages he paid.

My amateur boxing career was limited, but with some success (finals of Kansas City Golden Gloves in 1974). I decided to turn pro with some prodding from a local cop friend of mine. I sparred with a light heavy pro out at a Long Island gym where J.J. (the cop) had a connection and the trainer gave me a green light. I couldn't drive there daily, so I was introduced to the trainer/owner of the 14th Street Gym in New York City. I did well in the beginning and was offered an opportunity to fight for a well-connected manager after a couple of wins.

By this time, I was working at Tottenville High School in the special education program while putting in three or four nights at the bar. If significant money had been offered, I may have accepted; but with two jobs and no time, I stuck with Al Gavin at the 14th Street Gym. I would continue boxing to the age of 40. I made some money and loved the excitement of the live fights. There were no teammates, no time outs, and no place to hide in the ring.

I had no permanent health insurance until I joined the New York City fire department in 1983. You had to heal on your own and put up with aches and pains. In my football career I only separated a shoulder, broke an ankle and suffered two concussions; which is mild, by most standards. From boxing, I lost a front tooth, endured three severe concussions, and busted numerous ribs and my nose countless times. I had it fixed, but it could still use some work. The pain was worse after a boxing match because my head and ribs would throb for days, but I still had to work my regular job.

New York was a financial mess during the late seventies and early eighties and I was released as a regular teacher, but continued on as a long-term per diem. I would lose my benefits in the summer. I drove a cab to make ends meet and had to put up with getting stiffed and abused by customers. Most people look at cabbies as down-and-outers, and a well-to-do former classmate let his gal know I was a former football hero relegated to driving them to their social event. Nasty fares didn't bother me much because I was making a living and had bigger goals.

A couple of friends were city lifeguards for the pools and beaches, so I decided to earn money while I got some sun and worked out. You had to be in shape, so we ran and lifted on our breaks when not on chair duty. If I wanted extra money I would pick up a fight and sell tickets to my friends; from which I received a commission besides the guaranteed pay. I would get my lifeguard buddies jobs as security in different bars. I was always getting friends employment because it was the natural thing to do.

I secured employment driving a bus for the seniors at the Jewish Community Center. I worked two-hour shifts every other day. *Any way to make a buck, or I wouldn't be able to pay the rent!* I didn't last long at the J.C.C. because they wanted me for more hours. I couldn't fit it in with the teaching and bar work. *When would I rest?*

The pay for security is minimal, since you're nothing but a strongman, but the bartenders made a mint. I found the time to go to bartending school and had to invest two hundred and fifty dollars for the two-month weekly class. Romeo (owner and instructor) promised to help place you when you completed the course. It wasn't very hard and the first job he wanted to place me in was a strongman at a high-end club. I turned it down and ended up placing myself at a local restaurant/bar. Bartending is tough because you have to be a counselor, adviser, sounding board, and referee—among other things—in order to receive great tips. I did fine at the Esquire Club, but still remember keeping the club open for a middle-aged couple who owned a bar and they stiffed me after listening to their whining for three hours by my lonesome. *Never mind I was scheduled to teach in two hours that very morning.*

CHAPTER 11

Screen Actors Guild

Al Gavin (my boxing trainer) hands me an address after my workout. He wanted me to audition for the part of a boxer for a Vectra Carpeting print ad. I show the next day for the audition and to my surprise, I get the job. They ask me to sign a contract for which I will receive $200 for the two days. It happened to be Memorial Day weekend in 1980, but I didn't care. I needed the money, and two hundred dollars equaled a week's worth of teaching.

Call time was 9AM and I was prompt. They provided me with the boxing shorts and shoes, which were two sizes too small. I endured the pain for ten hours of shooting. I thought it would take but an hour, but I wasn't complaining because the director offered me a copy of the brochure for which I was posing. The next day was eight hours of the same, but they secured me shoes that fit. When finished, the director made certain to explain I was only to receive two hundred dollars. There was an older guy hired to pose as an announcer and he worked but two hours. I later learned he made three times more than me. The director paid me cash and turned me on to some agencies that might be able to use my blue-collar type in Manhattan.

A month later I received the brochure and decided to present myself to casting agencies. I offered Al forty bucks from the two hundred and he swallowed it like a vacuum. A buddy of mine came with me to apply for modeling positions. The first agency we visited was Gilla Roos on West 16th Street. The entire staff gave us the fish eye when we walked in the door. There were different types of representatives sitting at each cubicle, but they all enjoyed a view of the two big lugs. Gilla, herself, was standing and we both said without hesitation, "If this is the look you want, this is the look we have." Both of us expected rejection, but Gilla explained she liked our blue-collar persona and had us fill out waivers and personal stats. Another point she insisted on was that we not quit our day job.

She sent us out on go-sees (possible employment for print jobs) that very day as blue-collar workers for a Coke magazine ad. I showed Gilla the magazine brochure where I was featured, and she let me know I should have been paid a twenty-five hundred dollar minimum for that type of job. Now I knew why they were insistent my pay was two hundred dollars—*because I was a dumb boxer.* I was ripped off!

Once I was able to have my front tooth capped properly and did away with my Caesar hairstyle, I began to make some money. Gay photographers and industry personnel often hit on my type, and they were very up-front about it. No beating around the bush like I did with women. *Can I have your phone number?* was the first thing out of their mouths. I wish I had that kind of nerve with the ladies. I'm not gay, but marveled at how they shrugged off rejection. I found myself getting upset when ugly men would ask me out. *At least, be respectable-looking,* I laughed.

Gilla sent me for a Coke commercial audition and I landed the spot. When I showed for work at some studio on East 27th Street, a woman asked me if I was talent. I replied I was there for the commercial and she asked my name. "Yes, you are talent," she responded after checking her list. She gave me a maroon robe with Tab (the diet soda) printed on back. There was a whole production with four other principals and countless extras. You saw my face for a split second and the premise was we were all knocked out by Diet Coke.

I received a check from the agency for five hundred dollars a few weeks later. *Not bad for a day's work*, I surmised. Two weeks later I receive a two thousand dollar check. I ask my friend in the Guild about it and he explains they are residuals. Every time it ran, I would receive money. I ended up grossing about twenty grand and was required to join the Screen Actor's Guild, of which, I remain a member. I never put the effort required to make it big, but did make decent money to supplement my income in the future.

CHAPTER 12

A Career In Comedy

I invested a small fee for acting lessons and the instructor told me I was great and to resign. When I mentioned this commendation to my agent (David Roos), he kind of grinned. I knew something was up and asked, "She says that to everyone, right?" "Of course," David deadpanned. "She wants you to keep paying."

My brain was in overdrive and I decided to enlist in a comedy course for two hundred bucks. *I figured, how hard could it be?* because I would be interacting with people and making them laugh. This would help me with my acting [and] I would be the individual getting paid. It was a win-win. The course ran for a month and I was seen and interviewed by Steve Dunleavy from the New York Post for an article on the comic fireman. They taped my set and I received a lot of laughs. The first night I performed outside the class was for a cancer fundraiser at Rags To Riches on East 54th Street.

When I asked some friends to go, they were astonished and informed me *emphatically* it would be the most difficult thing I had ever done. I laughed, figuring I had played for the Giants and fought professionally, so this couldn't be more difficult. My friends were right (since I never figured on hecklers). I worked some big clubs like The Comic Strip, Dangerfield's, and The Improv. As a comic, I was clean and sometimes came out in tights so the world could tell I had been circumcised. The tough part of this business is practicing until you make it big. You have to work these low rent clubs *basically for free* until you become known, and the atmosphere is one of smoke and alcohol. Most of the time you would get home at three in the morning, and that would take a toll on workouts and the day jobs.

I had some laughs and heartaches, but gave it up after I had to drop one of the drunken patrons at a 'low life' club I was working. Here's how it went down:

I was furious at the heckler. He was ruining my show because he was inebriated and untalented. I asked him what he used for birth control, his personality? And he cussed some more as his buddies encouraged him.

I was but five yards from his table at the dive club I was working and told him that he is what happens when a fetus doesn't receive enough oxygen. When he continued ranting, I said if I wanted any more crap from him, I would step over and squeeze his head.

His entire table began berating me and I hollered they should all pool their IQ's together and come as one idiot next time. The man stood up and cussed me out and was directly in my face, so I dropped him with a hook to the body. And the pummeling began.

This gave me some notoriety in the world of comedy because it was something they always dreamed of doing, but couldn't afford to.

CHAPTER 13

Can I Dance?

I never had much rhythm, but when the male dancer fad for females-only (I can't stress this enough) came into being in the early eighties, I decided to give it a whirl. This was a way to meet women and get paid for it. You needed to have a gig. I remember speaking to a troupe owner by the name of Gregory by phone and he told me, "If you don't have an act, don't come up. If you have an act, get up here. We want some men with muscles. The women are tired of seeing the tall and skinny."

I decided to make an act for myself. Since dancing wasn't my forte, I cobbled together a skit where I dressed as a nerd and wore the pleated pants, shirt, tie, and Sears back-to-school sweater complete with wing tip shoes and argyle socks. A plaid book bag and Coke bottle glasses enhanced my geeky persona. I carried a radio and the M.C. would encourage the audience to beckon me to come on stage, since I was shy. I would play to the crowd and inch out a bit further the louder they became. I would eventually make it to a chair in the middle of the platform and turn on my radio. The tape enclosed would play like I was shifting radio stations until I found the right one, which played some up-tempo music. I would come out of my shell and strip off the clothes until I was in nothing but my Jockeys.

It was fantastic being admired by a throng of women having a ball while stuffing dollar bills in your briefs. I worked for Gregory for a while and then set out with my own bookings. For large shows I employed a few friends who could dance and were in fantastic shape, and did my solo gig for small parties and bridal showers. I teamed up with a woman who had her own stripping business and we would both perform at coed parties. The job lasted me about four years and I made a lot of cash, met a lot of women, and had more laughs than I could hope for.

One guy from the firehouse hired me for his fiancée's bridal shower, and a high school coach I knew booked me for his daughter's bachelorette party. I performed at surprise birthday parties for women in bars and restaurants.

An agent friend got me a $500 gig at the Rainbow Room for a corporate executive's birthday party. It was for his younger brother who took up white-collar boxing and I was hired to dress as a boxer and challenge him to a fight in the middle of the room. He was so frightened I had to make him hit me in order to go down. They were so rich, a Broadway ensemble was hired to sing for the party. I got to see how the bigwigs party; and made some nice cash to boot!

CHAPTER 14

Liquor Store Cashier

Every year since college the owner of Gene's Liquors on Staten Island would persuade a group of athletes to fight in local smokers for various charities. It didn't matter to him how much training or experience you had, as long as you would step in the ring with him in your corner. He professed to have a stable of fighters, just like the big-time promoters. I always enjoyed the challenge and competition, so I readily agreed. A poster of Rocky Marciano hung in his establishment signed by Rocky to three different people. Gene's name was included, but in different ink and of irregular script. A forgery if I ever saw one. He did provide me with employment as a store clerk when he had to step out in the evening, so I have added the job of liquor store sales to my repertoire.

CHAPTER 15

New York City Fire Department

In May of 1983, I was appointed and joined the greatest fire department in the world. Many of my friends were already members. Guys I knew from first grade, high school classmates, football teammates and neighborhood acquaintances were already on "the job," which was the name given to the fire department on Staten Island (the forgotten borough). I car-pooled with three new members I knew from athletics to the probationary school on Randall's Island. We had a ball interacting with the instructors and eating at the Greasy Spoon at 7AM while waiting for the day to begin. We had to leave Staten Island at 6AM to beat the traffic, so we always had time to kill on arrival. The heavyset individual who ran the food truck piled lard on the pan to an extreme. The food slid into the body cavity, and Michelle Obama would have declared his establishment off limits for contributing to heart failure.

Fire school was six weeks in duration. And upon completion, I began my career in Coney Island at Engine 245 and Ladder 161 on West Eighth Street. After a night tour, I would run the beach with fellow firefighters. This was a job where your heart rate can go from 60 to 180 in a matter of seconds, so it was imperative to be in top condition. A slow jog just wasn't feasible *if* you wanted to be the best firefighter in the world. My grade school buddy, Steve Lopez, broke me in for the engine work, and Jack Ronaldson (a buddy from football) helped me with truck work. My grade school basketball coach was my captain. We had bunks for the night tour, but I could never sleep since I was always preparing mentally for the next fire or emergency. You are only as good as your last fight, and I took this to heart in every job position I ever held.

Night tours ran from 6PM to 9AM, and day tours were from 9AM to 6PM. You were permitted to switch tours with other firefighters if you needed days off. The pension and health benefits were fabulous and the pay mediocre. I needed the second and third job to put money away for the future, as did almost every other firefighter. The first four years on the job I worked as a substitute teacher, exotic dancer for females, bouncer/ security, actor/model and volunteer football coach. I stopped teaching after my fourth year, but continued with the other jobs and added employment as a personal trainer, fitness class instructor, and international presenter. I would pick up an occasional professional boxing match when I had the urge for mayhem and travel.

A friend and probationary firefighter from my company became paralyzed from the neck down while working his second job clearing trees. He had two kids and was in his early twenties. Everyone was talking about how they were going to start projects for donations to help with his medical expenses. When nobody stepped up after two weeks, I went to Madison Square Garden and signed for a bout in which twenty percent of my ticket sales would go to Manny Demartinez (the injured party). I gave the money I made from the fight to Manny and had to collect the ticket money the night before the bout because nobody could assist from the companies. Sometimes people are a lot of talk, just like the politicians. They say many things, but it's all a lot of nothing.

Six months later, I fought in Atlantic City and the firefighters from Coney Island hired two buses to come and support me. I was required to be at the Atlantis Hotel and Casino the day prior for the press conference, and I regretted missing the bus ride because that was all the men in the company talked about the following two weeks. It was the best time ever, and the stories flowed like water from a faucet. The bus driver was so upset with their antics he refused to drive them back. That about sums it up without having to get into the dirty details.

The fight went as planned for me and I won, but the only drawback was not getting any sleep the night before because I shared a room with my trainer and he snored the entire night. My professional record was a satisfactory 7-5 when I retired at age 40.

Ace lands a big right in Atlantic City.

Dennis with Evander Holyfield.

In 1989, I began my career as a personal trainer/aerobic instructor. Dance classes weren't my style, so I taught a dynamic aerobic boxing class. I must have instructed at over fifty different gyms in New York City. Most were in midtown Manhattan, so the subway was my mode of transportation to save on tolls and gas for the car. I slept for the thirty-minute ride on the Staten Island ferry, and more than once failed to awake before the boat headed back to Manhattan from Staten Island. My classes were popular, since boxing was the rage, and I was known for a kick-butt, take-no-prisoners fifty minutes of absolute ferocity. If anybody didn't like the class, I promised to *clean their house for a week!* I taught fitness classes for eighteen years and never had to clean one home.

Many male aerobic instructors are gay and didn't like me intruding in their world, so they treated me like an outcast, but I found it amusing. One guy used more makeup than females and they provided me with material for a book. When I told the guys at the firehouse about the instructor I caught stuffing his jock strap with socks, they questioned whether I was homosexual—and had a lot of fun with it. You can't volunteer any personal information at the firehouse without the world knowing.

The Health and Racquet Club in New York City has seven clubs and I was employed at all of them for eighteen years. The pay was great and I met women that were in fantastic shape. It was better than going to clubs because I preferred athletic women who didn't smoke, and that constituted the majority of the gals in my class.

I parlayed the boxing craze into guest instructing at the most elite spas in the country (Golden Door in California, Canyon Ranch in Tucson and Massachusetts). They were like vacations. My guest and I would be treated as payees free of charge and I was required to teach my class once a day. Sandals at Montego Bay in Jamaica offered me the same deal for a week. The flight and travel were taken care of by the company.

CHAPTER 16

Guest Instructor at Golden Door Spa

This book wouldn't be complete without mention of my most memorable moment as a guest fitness instructor at the most elite spa in the U.S.A. I couldn't afford the price of $8,000 per week each guest had to pay. A stay at the Golden Door was a must for the rich and famous when considering a healthy, tranquil vacation. Each guest stayed in their own private villa and was treated like royalty for seven days. The grounds were incredibly beautiful and serene, while the views took your breath away.

I initiated the boxing program for guests in 1993, and for the next three years earned a guest experience for myself and one assistant in exchange for teaching a boxing class and the skills of the sweet science to their capable staff and guests.

In addition to enjoying all the healthy foods, which are grown in on-site gardens, I was treated to spa treatments I had only dreamed about. Collagen masks, manicures, pedicures, herbal wraps, facial and neck massages, use of a state-of-the-art fitness facility, and the infamous body scrub completed my itinerary. My boxing partner and former New York State heavyweight champ, Martin Snow, accompanied me on this trip. The rich and famous clientele . . . Josie Bissett from Melrose Place, her husband Rob Estes, Ted Gund of Gund Teddy Bear, Cliff Heinz of Heinz Ketchup (I asked for a job in his ketchup factory), Joan Lunden, brokerage owners, etc., . . . were mesmerized by the life and times of two regular blue-collar guys and sought out our advice on fitness and life's struggles.

In the middle of the week I was scheduled for my body scrub at the solarium immediately following my partner. As luck would have it, I was speaking to one of my new buddies and mentioned the body scrub to him. He informed me that he never participates in the treatment because a man scrubs down your entire naked body. After my massage I hightailed it out of the solarium, nixing the scrub delight. My partner admonished me later for not giving him the high sign about the experience.

With our new friends gathered around, Martin explained how he was instructed by Pete (the scrubber technician) to strip naked and lie on a morgue table. Martin happens to be 6'5" and weighs 260 lbs. The unnerving incident ensued where Pete used exfoliates to scrub his huge back for a meager five minutes while washing his behind for thirty uncomfortable minutes. Martin swore to all who were present how he now does not have to wash his behind for a month. The following afternoon Pete sought me out and was irritated I was a no-show for my scrub. I pleasantly declined, but could ascertain Pete was irritated I dismissed his work.

Another demeaning aspect of the scrub was that Pete hoses you down while standing completely naked in front of him. All I can say is, better Martin than me.

Back home, my boxing class was thriving. I was featured on *Good Day New York*, *The Today Show* and *Fox Five News*. My girlfriend (former ballerina who I met in one of my classes) and I conducted fitness workshops at gyms across the country.

I was asked to present at the I.D.E.A. International Fitness Expo at the Las Vegas Hilton in 1995. Only the best instructors in the world were invited, so I was humbly honored. I led my class from a stage platform attended by 400 of the best instructors in the world. They loved the class and my ratings were near the highest for a first-time presenter. The participants called me the *Real Deal,* but that name was already reserved for Holyfield.

My acting career continued during this tenure and I didn't find much time to rest, since I was getting numerous print jobs and commercials. I was booking some national commercials and my ugly mug was appearing in magazines, newspapers and billboards. The Diet Coke commercial I did with Evander Holyfield for the 1996 Super Bowl [and] an industrial for Pepsi with Angelo Dundee in 1984 both came about because of my boxing background. I had a featured role on two television programs and performed background work in a few movies. The fact I was a fireman and stayed in shape didn't hurt. In 1997, I was Mr. August in the beefcake calendar (FDNY Firehouse Hunks).

"They'll put anybody in those things," my police sergeant brother told me. The proceeds were donated to charity and we did signings at different landmarks around the city. My most embarrassing moment happened at Bloomingdales when, after signing for the one man in a throng of women, he grabbed my behind and got a free feel before sprinting away.

I turned down some lucrative offers for wealth during my fire career, but I loved the job and knew the pension benefits were secure. In 1997, I was offered a job working on the Chicago stock exchange—where you can make millions—and a recurring role as a bodyguard on the popular show, *New York Undercover*. The casting agent would never call me again and was stunned I would turn down such an opportunity. The firehouse was where I wanted to be!

In May of 2000, a gym buddy of mine named Paul Burnside secured me a job as the fire safety director of the Palace Hotel on 50th and Madison. He was second in command for hotel security and went out of his way to get me hired. I worked at the Health and Racquet Club on 50th and Madison two days a week and would immediately fulfill my duties at the Palace when finished teaching fitness classes. I received twenty dollars an hour for investigating fire hazards and teaching the employees fire safety. Paul let me double as hotel security if I wanted more hours. The job was intriguing and I learned from Paul how to detect hotel thieves. This man saved that hotel a lot of money with tireless investigating, and I was fortunate to earn a salary while learning the trade.

CHAPTER 17

Waterfront Boxing Gym

A buddy of mine opened a gym on New Street opposite the stock exchange and asked me if I wanted in. I invested some money and taught fitness boxing classes and booked personal training sessions. There was a lot of competition in the area, but we carved out a niche since we catered to the white-collar boxing crowd. The owner came up with an innovative idea called the "grudge match." When employees of the major investment firms had a specific dislike for colleagues, we would train them and conduct the bouts at our downtown gym. It made for a raucous night—and the combatants relieved their stress and defended their honor, while friends and fans drank, ate and cheered them on. It was a win-win for everyone and *I wish* our leaders would do the same. We all hear so much smack-talk from Democrats and Republicans. For once, I would like to see them sweat for a living and box, rather then spew vitriol at one another. They talk tough, but that's about it. Fight Cowards, Fight!

One young woman I trained to box was Leonie Lewis and she took a back seat to no one. If her husband would have let her turn pro, I could have made millions. She would spar with anyone and everyone and made Jeff Fenech (former world champ) from her native Australia proud.

CHAPTER 18

The World Changes 9/11/2001

As with any other day in my life, as a New York City firefighter I made certain to arrive at least thirty minutes before roll call to secure an early relief for anybody who desired or required such. Those who would report to the minute were called a variety of names, with none being very chic and most downright nasty. The house watch was on automatic and the buzzer sounded at Engine 156 as I opened the red door with our secret code. The key lock was more to my liking, but the forces that rule decided to go high tech. Disadvantages occur when relocated or detailed because you aren't familiar with the combinations. Nobody desires to be left out in the frost, and the chiefs making the rule should realize that a company has to vacate quarters in the course of duty.

I meticulously positioned my turnout gear near the rig to enable a rapid response. In the process, I heard a quick clamor of footsteps descending the creaking stairs to identify the unannounced intruder (it was I and he should have been able to identify such from the video camera in our third floor kitchen). The culprit was Anthony, who was relatively new, and he rapidly entered the computer cubicle to finish his thirty minutes. He gave me a quick hello and focused his eyes on the morning paper, which he had absconded from the third floor.

While ascending the stairs, I yelled if any individual wanted to leave since I was ready to ride. I deposited my wallet in the second floor locker I inhabited and dressed rapidly into regulation work shirt and trousers. I was always a stickler for uniformity and cohesiveness, but some firefighters would wear regular jeans and shirts with insignias not related to the fire department of New York. Some officers required they change to uniformity, while others were lax in this discipline and demonstrated some raggedness in their own dress.

My routine was like the hands on a clock and my next duty was to start a wash for my dirty gym clothes. The washer and dryer were situated in the second floor bunkroom, and after a minute preparation, I was arriving on the third floor for some firehouse banter on everything and anything. I could write a book on all the fantasy put forth from the kitchen table, and there might be something of worth on the television if conversation was nil. I was certain no job (working fire) had played out, as I would have sniffed out the smoky gear without any surprise. It could linger for the day like Right Guard on an underarm.

Willie (John Willardson) was in the T.V. room with his feet up on a lounger. I smiled while getting a cup of orange juice from the refrigerator. Manny Bracero (a relatively new firefighter of less than five years) had just returned from being detailed at Rescue 5 for the evening. He explained he was working the day with us and that Mike Fiore had relieved him early over in the Rescue. Lt. Obremski relieved his peer and was enjoying his coffee. While Manny was operating the remote, cryptically, the World Trade loomed large on the screen with smoke billowing from the upper floors. The newscaster did not have a clue and theorized a small plane had crashed into the landmark of capitalism.

The first fifth alarm sounded over our voice box at Engine 156 on Staten Island. Another one followed soon after, and all eyes were glued to the set like tar to a feather. I recalled thinking there is no way a small piper could cause the furnace enveloping numerous floors on the tallest building in New York City. A moment later this was confirmed—as a jet airliner crashed the second tower. Fifth alarms bellowed furiously from the dispatcher on our voice alarm. I contended we would be summoned and hurried down the aged wood after telling Manny to get prepared. I passed Ed Sweeney (called *Swiney* by Lt. Tyler, who was called *Lt. Titler* by firefighter Sweeney) and *Royal* (Roy) Smith, who were minute men (would arrive only minutes before their tours began unless you issued a special request previous), leisurely ascending the stairway. I stacked my turnout equipment on the engine and hurried back upstairs for a protein shake, knowing I would be without food for a long haul. As the last gulp splurged through my intestines, our immediate response was requested by our computer and we hastened to our assigned positions.

Sweeney was the chauffeur, Reilly nozzle, Bracero backup, Smith second backup, and Willardson the control. While only a ten-mile distance to the terror attack, traffic in New York City can make it hours. Gridlock materialized at the entrance to the Verrazano Bridge. Willie and myself exited the rig to direct vehicles aside to quicken our response. Mass confusion was already astride, since many were not attuned to the severity of this emergency. Once over the bridge we found our travel clearing—with full view of only one tower standing and fires roaring about. Time moved promptly until the Brooklyn Bridge, where we slowed to a trickle while merging with our fellow firefighters. The second pillar of private enterprise pancaked to its destruction, enlisting more fury for the already putrefied oxygen—as fear and panic followed the disheveled citizens fleeing the collapse. We mustered at city hall after taking leave of our engine at Chambers Street. We all started voicing our last requests with the chauffeur, Ed Sweeney (under the assumption he would remain with our engine), when orders came in that we would all be responding as a search and rescue team.

We hurried to Ground Zero, and chaos was far and wide with no command to be followed. We picked up an abandoned line and turned it on a burning window, but the pressure was futile. A chief I remember as Podlucky was pointing to a burning window while a tower ladder was saturating the structure. The team in the bucket obviously knew what they were accomplishing. And why this officer kept yelling and barking unnecessary directions seemed all so surreal. We met up with Tower Ladder 79, which is a company we normally respond, and saw Charlie

Van Pelt (CVP) who was detailed for the 9AM by 6PM tour from our company. He relayed how his officer kept demanding to be rerouted to the World Trade instead of their assigned relocation to a Brooklyn company. If the dispatcher had heeded his appeal, Charlie and the company would have perished.

We descended basements with abandoned hose lines, but the pressure was flatulent. Our searching went on without rest, but appeared futile, as you realized there were thousands upon thousands of pounds of burning debris, concrete, and steel pulverizing the humanity trapped within. There was no time to think about the enormity of this carnage on our soil, and most companies were on their own as far as search and rescue. While seemingly fruitless under the circumstances, you continued the hunt for possible survivors.

About five in the afternoon we took a breather for water and food in a blown-out grocery. Ed Sweeney started to cut some meat and I reminded him of the contamination. He redirected himself to some packaged food and made due, but the air was thick with fiendish particles and you had to eat fast to prevent them from invading your respite. We were operating in the vicinity of 7 World Trade and some tower ladders were hitting the stubborn flames that refused to die as I ventured into the lobby of a residential high-rise opposite the conflagration. Two residents happened down the stairs and asked me if it was safe to remain in the building. I explained how water and electricity would be scarce and the air quality was hazardous. If they had an alternative place to reside, they should seek safety there, or go uptown and stay at a hotel to get away from the epicenter. They thanked me for the concern and job we were trying to do.

I returned outside, united with our company, and we made our way to the partially destroyed quarters of 10 Engine and 10 Truck. They were located across a double lane of traffic from Ground Zero and a staging area was established for search and rescue within the remains. Off-duty firefighters, Pat Smith and Lt. Bob Burns, arrived in their gear to help with the search. Firefighters from all the boroughs were recalled and many arrived to help long before the official order. All of the rescue workers formed human chains to remove debris in the faint hope of locating survivors. The scale of what had occurred will never be realized or accepted by the individuals who responded. The digging seemed fruitless, and you would hear an occasional roar come from those closest to the removal. This turned out to be rescuers helping rescuers who had gotten injured and now were removed by stretcher.

Around midnight, first aid trucks arrived and staffers would come around to wash out our eyes. We were issued flimsy paper-like masks that were useless, since they stuck to your face and became filthy within seconds. I know they were issued with good intentions, but you could not work on the burning pile [once the World Trade] and use these with any efficiency.

Ace (seated with paper mask) takes a break during rescue operations.

Incessant fires burned beneath our feet, thanks to some Muslim extremists who hate our government. So many great men perished because of these cowards. I can say *great* without hesitation, as I knew many of them—and I hear this word thrown about to so many not as deserving.

About 1AM, I bumped into a friend of mine named Tom Henri, who was working in another company, and he began telling me of the friends we had lost. They were guys I had grown up with, went to grade school, played ball, worked outside jobs (most firemen have second jobs, since the pay is not exceptional), went to the beach, and had countless laughs throughout our times. Bill O'Keefe, Charlie Margiotta, Mike Fiore, John Fisher, Paul Mitchell, Charlie Kasper, Mike Weinberg (we were in the fireman's calendar the same year. He was good-looking and we laughed how they would put anyone in those things), Gerry Barber, Steve Siller (he was off duty and ran in his gear from the Battery Tunnel to the World Trade), John Bergin, Greg Buck, Brian Belcher.

You start to feel guilty immediately and it grows on you. Why them and not me? Charlie was on his way home and jumped on the rig of Rescue 5. Billy was training for captain at headquarters. They all went above and beyond and will never be forgotten. Mike Fiore had relieved Manny early that morning, so Manny was spared. They both had children. I played spirited basketball games against both Mike and his dad at the local Y. John Fisher and his family lived but five houses from the gym.

Our department took a huge hit that day. Pat Brown from Rescue Unit, who was a fireman's fireman, was lost. I attended his funeral at St. Pat's in Manhattan (we believed he probably made it the furthest up the tower because that is just how he performed). Chief Ganci, who was Department Chief (the big cahuna) refused to leave the tower until all his men were safe. He made the ultimate sacrifice, as did Chaplain Mychal Judge (a poor soul forced to jump from the red devil crushed him in his death dive). There are countless tales—and not enough manuscripts to hold them—of the 343 firefighters who gave their all that day while making the supreme sacrifice. All the rescue personnel and the citizens who were slaughtered are heroes from that cowardly attack. I cannot count the number of citizens who have told me I am a hero for my response that horrific day. The only people who deserve to be so honored are those who died.

At about two thirty in the morning we were told to return to quarters. There were buses at Chambers Street to transport the companies. Lt. O did a member check and Manny was missing. We searched the immediate region, but he was nowhere to be found. Thinking he may have gone on ahead, we tried to find our bearings to locate Chambers Street. No standing street signs were visible. I knew this area like the back of my hand, but it took awhile to find a proper direction. We were both numb and beat up and our exposed orifices were caked with grey globs of unknown elements. Our turnout gear was filthy for those of us who still had theirs. (Someone had borrowed Ed Sweeney's helmet and turnout coat and forgot to return them. It turned out to be an ambulance worker and they were reunited three months later. It was unfortunate for Ed, as the following day he was forced to search in a borrowed coat and a Con Ed helmet.)

We made the trek to a subway station at Chambers, but no buses were there. The Lieutenant was increasingly worried about Manny and we headed back to Ground Zero to locate our missing colleague. We continued a futile search for our misplaced rescuer, and then Lt. O recalled his cell phone was on his person. He immediately dialed our firehouse to find that Manny had returned to quarters with Pat Smith and Bob Burns.

[For lack of vehicular transport] we decided to walk the quarter mile to the Staten Island Ferry for our transportation back to quarters. We walked in eerie silence trying to comprehend what had taken place, but it failed to register in our soul of guilt and denial. Before anyone spoke, a police van happened by and asked our direction of choice. Roy informed him of the small trek to the ferry and they told us to hop aboard for a lift. The two officers inquired further of our destination, and upon being informed, offered to drive us to quarters. They had been on morgue duty and there was not much action, since the unfortunate heroes were entombed under tons of rubble. We thanked them and hunkered down in our seats recalling the unspeakable attack that had taken place.

For the first time in our lives, we were the only vehicle on the Brooklyn Queens Expressway. The bizarre emptiness continued en route to quarters. No one said much, since there was not much you could say. We did compare notes on rumors of the Sears Tower and the White House itself being hit, but other than that—not a word was spoken. The normally hour-long journey did not exceed twenty minutes, and we thanked our brothers in blue for the door-to-door service.

Our company was manned by firefighters from New Jersey, and we dropped off our gear and headed for home. My voicemail was satiated with concerned voices from friends and family and lifted the character of my deadened spirit. I only called my wife-to-be, as it was past four in the morning and I wanted to ascertain she was safe. She was a flight attendant for Continental Airlines, and reports were circulating of the atrocities committed against them by the Muslim extremist hijackers. She was at her home in Florida and doing fine, but it would be some days before she could fly back to New Jersey and continue her occupation.

I could not sleep, but reminisced about my lost brothers and lay staring at the darkness for three hours after a shower. Life as it was before September 11 ceased to exist, and I embarked for the firehouse at eight in the morning. We mustered and were transported by bus with other companies to continue our search and recovery. There were no commands of consistency, and we went to dig and search with our own group from the company.

The individuals of this great country showed their true grit. There were volunteers flowing in from every corner of the United States of America. Steel workers, plumbers, laborers, private industry, welders, first aid, and every occupation imaginable offered assistance. From Pennsylvania, Virginia, California, Ohio, Indiana, and every other state, Americans were donating their time and money to help New York City. Where help and food were sparse in the immediate aftermath, Americans were dashing to the rescue. You turned around and someone was offering you a hoagie and a beverage. Anything you needed was provided. It lifted our spirits for the moment. The residents of America demonstrated their true mettle. Nothing was organized and they came on their own, got down in the pit and dug with the rest of us. These people all led by example. So much was made of Rudy Giuliani coming down to Ground Zero at two or three in the morning on September 12 because of concern. I was there—he traveled by air-conditioned limousine and surveyed the situation. He did not get out and dig or perform any hands-on effort. No sweat was emitted from his brow. The people coming to aid us did it of their own endeavor. They did not need to be led. They were leaders by doing.

The funerals and memorials began shortly thereafter and brought me down to the lowest of lows. The grief on the faces of all the widows with young sons and daughters at their sides can bring the strongest of wills to severe depression. Our firefighter brothers and sisters came forth once again to assist at the funerals. There were three or four funerals a day on occasion with the churches within miles of one another. I can remember the formation outside of Mike Fiore's memorial consisted of firefighters from Canada, California and New Jersey—amongst others —in full dress uniform [to demonstrate] respect for the family and our fallen hero and friend. The constant mourning took a toll on everybody. The grieving process is ongoing. All of the heroes left their score on the ledger—and the country has suffered on account of it.

When I observe the hypocrisy of our country (mourning for weeks the loss of a politician, an entertainer, or some activist, while the pillars of our society sacrificed all and don't receive similar accolades), it resonates the bizarre behavior of politicians. Our soldiers take up the fight our politicians have delivered—and scarcely a word is spoken of their honor, sacrifice and bravery! Instead, we hear the terminology of the bullies and cowards running the country. Bush, Cheney, Frank, Pelosi, Reid, Obama, and the rest of the political spectrum are one-way entities. Why the media focuses on these morons and not the souls in the trenches *demonstrates the greed and maliciousness of those in command.* One trait they do foster is corruption. The two-party system orchestrates a blame-game-mentality as they pillage the taxpayers. We need a third party. If the individuals who sacrificed themselves on September 11th were running this country, you would have people putting the nation first and themselves second; rather than the continuous status quo of politicians first and country second!

After a week, we finally secured our rig back at quarters and resumed the rigors of our noble profession. Counseling was available, but conversing with those who shared the same duties was your guide through the continuous mind struggle. I can remember all the wakes and funerals I attended with solemn clarity. One in particular was that of Charles Margiotta, who went to the same grade school as myself. He was a man's man and spoke his mind on all issues with utmost clarity. On occasion, this could be detrimental because of his coarse vocabulary. Some bosses did not favor his mouth, but were too timid for confrontation. His dad (whom I had known since a kid) told me, "Boy, he was a piece of work." That said it all, and I will always remember Chuck as a piece of work.

At the wake of Greg Buck, a firefighter who worked briefly at our company, I felt particular sorrow for his wife-to-be and good friend, Cathy Morrison. Her words still resonate as to how she finally met the perfect guy and he was lost forever. What is forever branded in my character is how all of these heroes treated people the same way they wanted to be treated. It is so simplistic; yet, faithfully accurate.

CHAPTER 19

Hands-On Fundraisers

After the towers fell, Americans from all corners of the country contributed in some fashion to assist those who required the most assistance. *"All gave some and some gave all"* is the slogan I admired most. I'm still not able to comprehend all the friends and colleagues I lost that day. Going to funerals on a daily basis, digging and searching at the pile, and continuing my career at the firehouse brought sorrow and strength to my body. I wanted to contribute hands on to help the spouses and families of those lost.

When a New York City police buddy of mine informed me the N.Y.C. Police Department was organizing a smoker (charity boxing match for 9/11 victims) and they had no one to fight their heavyweight, I volunteered. On April 11, 2002, I came face-to-face with my opponent. He was known as the "White Rhino," 6 ft. 290 lbs. and about thirty years of age. None of the other cops wanted to fight him because he was super strong (qualified for worldwide strong man contests) and had recently beaten the Irish police champ. We both wanted to win and I came right at him with my broken nose. (I was sparring a few days earlier with my corner man, Martin Snow, who broke my nose.) I landed a left-right-hook combo before he caught me with a big right hand. I was up at six, but my corner halted the bout to my dismay. It wasn't the ending I envisioned, but the cause made up for it.

Maryann Donner, who is the program coordinator at New York Health and Racquet Club, promoted and designed a four-hour workout tribute for all those lost in the World Trade Center tragedy. I contributed by leading a one-hour boxaerobics class. One of my students, Ally Mathias, took over my boxaerobics class for months so I could devote more time to the fire department. Maryann Donner saw fit to mobilize the Health and Racquet Club on Whitehall Street to supply shower facilities for those participating in search and rescue. Maryann is an ace, and her efforts to help those families who lost loved ones was incredible.

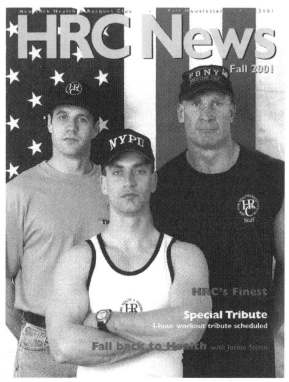

Dennis Reilly standing to the right.

On September 19, 2002, there was one more bout to be fought for the widows and orphans at Keyspan Park in Coney Island. It was New York Police against New York Fire, and (once again) I came out on the losing side. We won as a team, but I lost my bout. I thought I could beat anybody—even if they were twenty years my junior—and I took offense to those who joked about me losing when they would never have the courage to step in a ring; but I was happy they contributed to such a worthy cause. *Next time you donate money, see if there are opportunities to perform hands-on assistance. The inner rewards cannot be described.*

CHAPTER 20

Volunteer Board Member

Cindy, firefighter friends, and the gym maintained my sanity for the next couple of years until retirement in 2003. I was having problems with my lungs, and my left shoulder was in a constant state of surreal pain. After twenty years I retired, and Cindy and I decided to move to her home of twenty years—Parc Village Condominium—in Plantation, Florida. We married and settled in for a life of peace and prosperity. The first two years in Florida were fine, aside from the hurricanes. This is when a sordid story of deceit and deception invaded our simple life.

The Management Company running the machinations of our condo complex was indifferent, at best—and arrogant to an extreme, at worst. The owner thought we paid him so we could serve him (similar to the attitude the government has towards us taxpayers). The seven-person board didn't hold him accountable—and let him run our complex like we were his serfs. I decided to donate my time and ran for office in the upcoming elections. I wondered if I was doing the right thing when I heard some other individuals running for office bashing the people serving. If they felt comfortable smearing people behind their back, I was certain it could *and would* be me somewhere down the road.

My worst fears were justified when I was elected to serve with three new individuals. Instead of polling the homeowners and serving the will of the community, these spanking new office holders sought retribution against former volunteers while passing their own agenda. It was tough to comprehend the filthy rhetoric and tactics they used to attack those who stood in their way. The newly elected hired a new property manager, who turned out to be slicker than the previous fellow. *Is there a government official or property manager alive who is honest?* I have yet to find that individual.

I fought their acidic agenda every step of the way. Their leader used rules of radicals against me to perfection. Isolate and attack was the mantra and their dirty work was done as a mob. In a one on one, they were plain and simple cowards. When they tried to discredit a lone homeowner, I stuck up for his right to free speech, and we both sued this motley crew for defamation and slander. We had witnesses and evidence proving our case, so they settled out of court. *Am I wrong in guessing they didn't feel comfortable lying under oath?* I resigned shortly thereafter because I couldn't stomach the deceit and greed in which they operated. Shortly after I stepped down, this infamous group voted and gave themselves an allowance, reimbursed gas mileage and cell phone bills. Whatever happened to the word volunteer? If I had a nickel for every lie this group of individuals told, I'd be a rich man today. Before resigning, I called each one a liar, coward, and hypocrite to their face.

CHAPTER 21

Gym Sales in Florida

I had to get a job because that is what you are supposed to do. Why would I want a handout from Joe Biden, Barack Obama, George Bush and Dick Cheney? I'm better than them, so I wouldn't. We're all better than they are! If you look at their history, they attained prominence because of family money and stronger connections than the rest of us. If you'll take note, they all came into office with a large bank account and exited (or will leave) with an even larger one. When they lie to the American people that they feel our pain, it could only be true if they chose to live like us. And that, my friends, will never happen. On their best day and my worse, I will outwork the above-mentioned aristocrats and their devilish cronies.

Bally's was looking for sales help, and that was right in my wheelhouse. Besides being a part owner of the Waterfront Boxing Gym in New York, I learned from the best in the city. His sales numbers were staggering and New York Health and Racquet Club was the beneficiary. Tom Dinatale was his name, and he took me under his wing to show me the business when I became involved with Waterfront. Tom could sell granite to the jewelers in the diamond district, if so possessed.

I'm in my fifties and suffering from decreased pulmonary function and severe shoulder and hip arthritis, but I landed the job. It didn't last long because

I had a 20-year-old kid ordering me to consult with him before I closed a sale. The out of shape, sloppily dressed miscreant didn't know how to close. I could have taught him some things, but decided to leave gracefully. My supervisor, who was younger (but closer) to my age, was upset I was departing, but knew I would have a tough time working with twenty year olds.

Watching members perform in fitness classes gave me the urge to instruct once again, so I willed myself to endure the pain and began instructing at the local Plantation gym where I was a member. My classes were packed, but the pay was way off from what I received in New York City. To supplement the schedule I began training gym members for boxing and overall fitness. I took a sales position at the gym, but was let go after showing up the manager and his assistant. Just because I ran around helping everyone (like you should), management took offense. I made them look bad. The name of the establishment was Fitness First, and independent trainers and instructors (like myself) helped the members, while management worked themselves out! The franchise owner was stationed in Maryland and had no idea the paid staff took protein drinks and water without paying. Ah, what's a few dollars here and there, the manager figured? He was the owner's best friend. The gym ended up failing, but not soon enough for me.

With my health suffering, I discontinued teaching classes, but continued training members. Unfortunately, for me, I was about to meet pure unadulterated evil in the flesh.

The year was 2006. They hailed from Argentina and made themselves out to be pillars of the community. Carlos and Ema owned a million dollar home with built-in theater, imported Italian tile, heated pool, state-of-the-art kitchen, and a game center that resembled an arcade for their sixteen year old. The cabal would sucker anybody they could into their *money investment business*. Carlos was the husband and patriarch, happily married to wife, Ema, with children Patricio (16-year-old son) and Alejandro (older son of 25). Sharon was the wife of Alejandro and 23 years of age; and Ron, the brother of Sharon, all played a significant role in the scheme.

This family lived the new American dream. *In lieu of working, you can buy a million dollar home with no money down, own four luxury vehicles, eat the finest foods, wear the priciest clothes, go to the best schools, and not have to work!* Sharon did have a part-time job at a CVS, but no one else toiled unless you consider "graft" working.

I was requested to train the entire clan in the middle of 2005. Ema called my home after taking a class I was teaching. My respiratory problems were increasing, but I regretfully agreed because another instructor said they were the "nicest family." They trained three to four times a week under my tutelage. My wife and I began socializing with the clan, and after about a year Carlos and Ema asked if I wanted to invest with them. *"They normally don't take friends as clients, but would make an exception for us,"* was the pitch presented.

I sat down in the office at their million-dollar home and Carlos showed me a docket of the companies that invested with them. He had contracts and cancelled checks from police organizations and local communities, which proved good forgeries. He said they invested in foreign oil, foreign real estate, local real estate, and utilities and yachts. Their family owned seven corporations.

Cindy and I considered them our best friends and we dined at their home, invited them to ours, watched Pay-Per-View in their home theater, and were in regular contact three to four times per week. Ema boasted how their home in Argentina was so spacious and luxurious that she employed a cleaning staff of twenty. On Mother's Day 2007, Carlos surprised Ema with a brand new BMW for $60,000 cash. Anything Patricio pined for he received, and it was the best money could buy. Patricio lived in Plantation, but despised Plantation High School because it had a large black student enrollment. Carlos somehow got him into Cypress Bay High School in Weston when they weren't granting new admissions for students from their own district because of overcrowding. The sky was the limit. And this crew bought the best money could buy!

Sharon boasted how she was going to make big money working for Carlos in the summer of 2007. Alejandro took two weeks off for a business and pleasure trip abroad. He claimed the family had some kind of oil deal in progress. Carlos, Ema and Patricio took a trip to Vegas where they stayed on the strip at New York-New York Hotel & Casino, and later that summer the entire family enjoyed a group vacation to New York City in a travel van purchased by Carlos. While there, they visited a gym that I was affiliated with in New York City where I made sure they were treated like royalty. They contacted me while in New York City and thanked me for the workout my former partner personally administered.

After they returned from their fantastic vacation, I began to see all the red flags. By this time, I had been invested with *Money Investment & Business, Inc.* for eight months. My meetings with Carlos were always conducted with his son, Alejandro, because Carlos was not fluent in English, nor I in Spanish. The family gushed proudly that Alejandro was a genius just biding his time for a top position with the federal government. He claimed to be a computer genius and sent me investment opportunities through their website. Their website domain was *Money Investment & Business, Inc.* and they owned another company called *Handyman For Rent, Inc.*

My friend Karmen (also a Fitness First member) was hired by Carlos to work as his personal assistant. She wound up investing over $160,000 with the family and was coerced into taking a second mortgage on her condo. Ema was jealous of the younger and prettier Karmen and refused to let her assist Carlos in the home office. She worked at his warehouse, which contained some vans, but absolutely no business or employees except Karmen. Carlos was vying to get into her pants and even produced a document stating he was divorced. I was alarmed and asked Carlos for my tax documents for the investments, since I had been issued dividends of about two thousand dollars. He said not to worry, that he had a good accountant. Not liking his response, I told him I wanted my principal ($70,000) back immediately. Alejandro answered in the affirmative for his dad and advised the funds would be wired back into my bank account on a set date.

As anticipated, the money was never deposited into my bank account as promised, so I called Carlos to meet me at my bank. In an attempt to show his *good faith*, Carlos showed up with son Alejandro at his side. At that time, the bank vice-president (Alexandra) personally informed Carlos and Alejandro that the money was never wired into my account. In turn, Carlos wrote me two checks: $70.000 for the principal [and] $4,500 for the dividend. I deposited them promptly and Alejandro apologized for the inconvenience. I also have to note that while speaking with Alexandra, Carlos tried to put some moves on the pretty and petite bank executive, while boasting that he owned a television station and a financial empire. What a joke!

By this time, Karmen and I were comparing notes. She informed me that a friend of hers, Giocanda Diaz (who she encouraged to invest $50,000 with Carlos), was being pressured into investing another fifty thousand. Carlos offered her a piece of his handyman business and said they were making millions. The family claimed to have offshore oil investments, bought up foreclosed homes and resold them, and did work for the FBI. The Valencias also told me they owned an entire block of homes in exclusive Plantation Acres. I told Karmen to instruct Giocanda (Gio) to hold off on investing any more money with Carlos; that I would let her know if my checks cleared. Sure enough, both checks were returned "insufficient funds" from Carlos' bank, Washington Mutual. My stomach-wrenching fears became a reality: Carlos was planning on returning my funds by using Gio's newly invested fifty thousand dollars to continue the family ponzi scam!

The loving, adorable Valencia family dropped out of site. I called all the phone numbers that I had for Carlos and Ema, but no one returned any of them. I left messages pleading to them that this was my life savings and to please let me know what was transpiring.

On September 26, 2007, two days after a raucous condo board meeting, I drove to the Valencia home, carrying a note in hand. When I arrived at the home, Gio was there. She explained to me that she had been there for fifteen minutes and no one was responding. We saw Ema's BMW in the driveway. I knocked and rang the doorbell, but received no answer. I slipped a note under their door asking for *someone* to please contact me, since Cindy and I thought them to be friends.

At that time, I realized Gio had gone around to the back of their house. As it's a large house, I knocked on the door and rang the doorbell one last time. While I was walking back to my car, I overheard two women arguing back and forth in Spanish. I remained standing there, trying to understand their Hispanic rantings for approximately five minutes. Gio reappeared from behind the spacious home, hollering that Ema and Patricio Valencia were indeed home and had been arguing with her out back. She also said they had called the police—*which I thought was a good thing.*

A few seconds later, three Plantation P.D. patrol cars arrived on scene. The first officer to appear (Officer Joel Stevenson) ordered me to freeze and put my hands on the car (Ema's shiney, new BMW). I complied immediately. Before I could open my mouth, he informed me not to speak. He walked right past Gio (who had spoken and argued with Ema and Patricio) and did nothing. The officer continued straight towards me and ordered me to put my hands behind my back. I complied and he yanked my arms over my head, causing extreme pain to my left shoulder, cuffing one hand. *(I suffer from severe arthritis in my left shoulder and right hip, and have respiratory illness from my twenty years of service as a New York City firefighter and a first responder on 9/11/2001.)* He then brought my other hand behind my back and cuffed it. I have never had handcuffs on before and they were digging into my bones. I asked him to loosen them because it was causing extreme pain. He said they were as loose as he could get them, and he had to talk to Ema and Patricio inside the house.

By this time there were ten police officers on the scene. I pleaded with them to please loosen the handcuffs. I was standing there doubled over in pain, my breathing was labored. I thought I might collapse. One officer behind me was taunting me saying, "You're a boxer, you should know what pain is." He was behind me, but since I was doubled over, I could see his hand on either his gun or his baton.

After approximately five minutes, Officer Stevenson came out of the house and said to me that I couldn't come back there anymore. I could hear two other officers behind me laughing at my situation. Officer Stevenson began to uncuff me, informing me that his key didn't work [as] he jiggled the cuffs digging into my wrists. He then advised he couldn't "do it" and asked another officer to uncuff me, which he does. I thanked the officer. Officer Stevenson then asked for my I.D., which I explained was in my car. He pointed for me to retrieve it, and as I began to walk, the same officer who abused me stuck his leg out in front of me. I looked at Stevenson, and he told the officer to let me retrieve it after the officer had stopped me with his leg. The same officer followed me to my car, and I retrieved my wallet from the glove compartment. As I fished for my license, he saw my badge and asked what it was for. I told him I'm a retired FDNY firefighter, and he gave me a look of disgust. I mentioned that my dad and two of my brothers were NYPD and that I've never been cuffed before. Again, he gave me a look of disgust.

I asked the officer for permission to speak to Ema Casa Valencia, who I thought was my friend. I asked them to look at the note I had just left under her door. He didn't respond. That's when Ema marched out of her residence. Still believing she was a friend (I trained and socialized with them for eighteen months), I said to Ema, "What's going on?" She acted like she never met me before, and proceeded to tell me to "never come back on her property;" acting like we were never friends. She stormed back into the house. Her son, Patricio, would not come out of the house. *(A few weeks earlier, I had just given Patricio a football for his birthday when my wife and I were invited to the Valencia home for his birthday party.)* I again asked Officer Stevenson to retrieve the note that I left under the Valencia door—which explained everything—and he refused. He instructed Gio and I to leave and not come back.

I have two friends who are Plantation police officers. Both are outstanding cops and individuals, Joe Alu and Marty Hommel. I asked the officers who cuffed me not to tell Joe or Marty about this because I was embarrassed about being handcuffed. They laughed and said they would tell them, and then said, "We're just kidding." There were about ten police officers at the scene that evening. Most were very professional, except the one officer who cuffed me and wouldn't listen to me, and the other two who were laughing at me and mocking me.

A few days later a sheriff came to my house serving me with an "Order Setting Hearing on Petition for Injunction for Protection against Repeat Violence." The Valencias sure know how to work our justice system. (Gio was also served with an order against her.)

On October 10, 2007, I appeared in Court. Gio and I represented ourselves without an attorney (pro se). I brought four witnesses with me to testify on my behalf. Through the aid of her son Patricio, Ema wrote an injunction statement against me. It wasn't until I read her statement that I—along with practically the whole City of Plantation—learned that her real name was not Ema Casa Valencia, but it was Ema Paolazzi. In her statement she claimed being *divorced* from Carlos Casa Valencia for two years (which was also new to me because they portrayed themselves as a happily married couple). She also claimed that, "My son and I don't know this person (meaning me) too well" and that I (myself) threatened to "pound" their faces in, and that she and her *ex-husband* Carlos didn't live together.

Of course all of her statements were later proven in court to be flat out perjury. However, it wasn't that easy. The presiding Judge was all set to grant Ema's order of protection against me before even reading her statement. In the early stages of the hearing he was selectively only listening to Ema and Patricio's lies because they had an attorney representing them—who, by the way, was retained by her estranged husband Carlos Casa Valencia. Just before the Judge was ready to sign on the dotted line, I told the Judge that I had witnesses and documentation with me that would prove the Valencias just committed perjury in open court. I also had proof that they lied in their written statement against me. He responded, "I'm not interested in that report." I reminded him that 'that report' was the injunction against me, the very reason why all of us were in the courtroom.

That was the turning point when he finally decided to look at my evidence—which included voluminous pictures of social gatherings with the Valencia family and testimony from my witnesses (one of whom was a Plantation police officer). After I was given an opportunity to present my evidence and witnesses, Judge Krathen *finally* saw the light and dismissed the injunction for protection against both me and Gio. In fact, Judge Krathen said he believed Ema and Patricio were lying on the stand about their allegations. *Considering their blatancy of lies on the record, they should have been charged with perjury, but no one did anything.*

In follow up to my altercation with the Plantation police in September of 2007, and after relocating to North Carolina in September of 2009, I finally received a copy of the police report from the original incident after vigorously trying for three years. Upon reviewing the report, I learned that Officer Joel Stevenson went back to the Valencia residence and advised Ema 'Paolazzi' to file an order of protection against me. I also learned that the officer who swore to the validity of Officer Stevenson's report was not at the scene in September 2007. *How do I know this?* Because that officer was a personal acquaintance of mine at the time and told me he wasn't at the scene.

CHAPTER 22

Spit Shined Vincent

I was upset about my treatment by the Plantation Police Department, so I called internal affairs officer Sgt. Richard Vincent and voiced my complaint. After explaining how I was cuffed and treated by the officers, he had a negative answer for everything. "You misunderstood the men and perceived them wrong. Cuffing is normal procedure." *I thought to myself, wow, Vincent must be a psychic since he wasn't present.*

He asked me if I won the order of protection complaint against me, and when I answered affirmatively he said, "You won, so drop it!" I could consider this a threat, but ignored him and explained that I did not want this to happen to others, so I'm proceeding with my complaint. I told him I would like a copy of the report, and his response was, "In my thirty years of law enforcement I've found you don't need it," and advised he would have a supervisor call me. *Vincent knows everything because he sat behind a desk for thirty years, I surmised.* Vincent further commented, "You know, we're not Podunk U down here." I replied I knew two Plantation cops who did a great job and considered them friends (we worked out together at the local gym). Vincent's smart-ass reply was, "Everybody knows them" in a sarcastic tone (implying I didn't know them, but was name-dropping). He told me he would have Stevenson's supervisor call me.

I did my homework on this man and found out he gets all spit shined up and gives instructions to Broward Sheriff's Department recruits. BSO recruit (Nick D.) once told me that he arrives in full uniform with his brass and shoes spit shined like he is God's gift to the world; and after his lecture he issues a test [which] was never graded and returned.

In my second phone conversation with Vincent in reference to my complaint (he never investigated), he informed me a Broward Deputy had been killed. The way he said it implied to me he does the same job as those in the field. Nothing could be further from the truth, and it saddens me when a slacker attempts to lump himself in with the brave cops working in the field. It so happened I was going to the fallen officer's funeral, so I mentioned that I would see him there, at which time he said he wasn't going because he had something going at the office.

Although I never met Sgt. Vincent, my vision of him is a guy who sits behind a desk and lumps himself in with the brave officers who put their lives on the line in the field. *However, he does spit shine his shoes and brass!*

CHAPTER 23

Lt. Bruce Finney

Sgt. Vincent did have Stevenson's supervisor call me at 7AM the next morning. His name was Lt. Bruce Finney. After he issued every excuse in the book for his officers (Stevenson and the punk whose identity they continue to hide), I informed Finney I still wanted the report and would like to come in and point out the men he should investigate. Finney informed me that I can't have the report or the names of the officers—and there was no way I would ever be allowed to see his men. He also added, "I thought you were going to be a nice guy about this." His excuse for the welts on my skin and my bloody wrists was because they were large *like his* (note, we never met) and the cuffs didn't fit. He is another man I would like to face in a boxing ring, but he would never have the courage to walk up those three steps. Finney is nothing more than a coward hiding behind a gun and a badge.

In follow up, I called Sgt. Vincent back and relayed my conversation with Lt. Finney to him. I later found out that Sgt. Vincent never filed a report. Furthermore, he never informed me that *by law* he is required to allow me to come in and fill out a complaint—of which, he is required to investigate.

CHAPTER 24

Detective William Tighe

In October of 2007, Giocanda (Gio) Diaz, Karmen Adame, and myself filed grand theft charges—via Plantation Police Department—against the Valencias amounting to over $250,000. I called the detective (William Tighe) who was assigned to our case to schedule an interview and I was greeted with an agitated, "I already have too many cases." *I did not want to hear this from the man assigned to bring us justice after being ripped off for $70.000!* He reluctantly set a date for Gio (robbed of $50,000), Karmen ($165,000), and myself to meet with him in late October 2007.

We provided Detective Tighe with documentation, photographs, and personal testimony as to the involvement of the entire Valencia family (Carlos, Ema, Alejandro, Sharon, Patricio—and Ron Montesdeoca, who claimed to be Sharon's brother) concerning the theft of our monies. We also provided him with information as to other victims who had been pilfered to the tune of $700,000. For many of these individuals it was their life savings.

Tighe wrote things down, made copies of our documentation, but never provided us with a report from that meeting; nor gave us any updates on the progress of the case. In November and early December—a time period of four weeks—I left several phone messages, but he never returned any of them. *As the Valencias remained free to conduct their scam and prey on more innocent victims!!*

CHAPTER 25

Interview at State Attorney's Office

The Valencia case sat idle for over a year, but thanks to investigative news reporter Carmel Cafiero (you'll hear more about her in coming chapters), the pressure is on the Plantation P.D. to act on my behalf. Detective Tighe is now resigned to interview me about the Valencia case at the State Attorney's Office. State Attorney Jeff Morris called me to set up the meeting. I found it odd that Tighe would meet with me now after having been given this information more than a year prior.

The meeting was recorded and began with Tighe—a smirk on his face—questioning whether I had been arrested on the date in question (September 26, 2007). *He was privy, of course, to what his buddies did to me back then; and subsequently, an untrue rumor spread at my condo complex that I was arrested for domestic violence.* I answered no, of course, and he proceeded to ask the same questions about information I provided him with a year earlier. What a farce! He acted like he had never seen me before. Talk about a man without a conscience.

A couple months go by after our state attorney meeting and, once again, I never heard from Detective Tighe. Annoyed and tired of waiting, I e-mailed police chief Larry Massey and voiced my displeasure. He notified Tighe's supervisor, Captain Erik Funderburk, who contacted me and said that he was familiar with *my situation* and was sending Detective Tighe to my home for a photo I.D. of Carlos Casa Valencia. This was mind boggling because I gave Detective Tighe photographs of the entire family back in 2007.

During our conversation Captain Funderburk informed me that the reason I was cuffed in the September '07 incident was because I am a "large man." It did not matter that the family lied about the allegations against me or that I offered no resistance to the officers' demands. So one can assume that if you reside in Plantation and you're a large person, you *will be cuffed and abused* (size discrimination?). When I informed the captain about Lt. Finney telling me, "I thought you were going to be a nice guy about this," the captain explained that he wasn't going to get into 'semantics' with me.

On December 22, 2008, Detective Tighe and his partner came to my home. It was obvious he had a chip on his shoulder for calling his boss. He demonstrated such as he and his partner (both armed) behaved like I was the criminal. He let it be known that I shouldn't have complained about him. *I thought, the audacity of this man coming into my home pissed off because I complained about him not doing his job. It really made me wonder.*

The two officers made me feel uneasy. All they had to do was pick a fight, shoot me, and claim it was self-defense. I didn't trust anyone from that department, other than Joe Alu and Marty Hommel (we worked out together at the local gym and both men kept in tip top shape for their profession). Ignoring Tighe's annoyance, I went through with the charade of identifying the proper photograph of Carlos Casa Valencia. Tighe had his armed partner perform the photo I.D. while he stood behind me. He even attempted to fool me with decoy pictures.

I didn't hear from Tighe again until I voiced my displeasure (once again) to Captain Funderburk. While respectful, the captain was constantly making excuses for his guy. "He has a heavy workload. He was having a bad day." No progress report, no return phone call, no police report! (In New York City, detectives give crime victims a progress update every three weeks.)

This guy could do anything he wanted, so what would stop him from coming to my home and shooting me? Absolutely nothing! So I moved my family to North Carolina.

Update: Tighe did finally send me an e-mail putting Carlos in Argentina, while Captain Funderburk had him traveling to Panama!

CHAPTER 26

Carmel Cafiero To The Rescue

Lucky for us, investigative T.V. reporter Carmel Cafiero (an ace) took an interest in our misfortune. Up to this point we were denied due process *until* she forced the police into action by the scrutiny she was giving our case. Thanks to this I-don't-take-no-for-an-answer human dynamo of a human being, we learned that Detective Tighe and the Plantation P.D. have concluded that Carlos Casa Valencia has only committed a *MISDEMEANOR!* Now I know why Tighe wasn't returning my phone calls or providing me with a report. Jeff Morris from the State Attorney's Office informed me that Plantation police had "dropped the ball" because the charges should have been felonies from the get-go. On the other hand, Plantation P.D. was blaming the state attorney. My bets are on Mr. Morris.

On July 8, 2008, Carmel featured Gio, Karmen and myself on her show, ***Carmel on the Case,*** via WSVN-TV 7NEWS (even our dog Suki had a few seconds on the air). This resulted in other Valencia victims surfacing:

(1) Angel Rivera – He and several of his friends lost over half a million dollars;

(2) Unknown number of illegal aliens – Lost between $8,000 to $10,000 for the promise of a green card (Carlos loved preying on them);

(3) Ruth Hipp – Scammed for more than $40,000 in June 2008.

Detective Philip Toman assured Carmel on her show, which aired on local T.V., that the Plantation Police Department was investigating the entire Valencia family:

Detective Philip Toman: "We have three victims in the city that we are working on, and we are currently investigating Carlos Casa Valencia and his family for investment theft."

This statement turned out to be untrue because the victims were never called and the Valencia family was never questioned.

[The video clip of Carmel Cafiero's investigative report is no longer available. However, you can view the entire transcript by going to: http://www.wsvn.com/features/articles/carmelcase/MI90759/]

Thanks to Carmel Cafiero and State Attorney's Jeff Morris and Monte Herrera, the charges against Carlos Casa Valencia were upgraded from misdemeanors to six (6) felonies. Currently, Carlos has an outstanding warrant for his arrest for failing to appear in court to face the charges. In the meantime, Gio and I found out where the Valencias moved, the new gym where they were working out, who had jobs, and the many banks Carlos and Ema ripped off. It was a flim flam.

Carmel staked out his new abode in an exclusive gated community on Diamond Terrace in Davie, Florida and caught him on camera depositing the trash in the early morning hours. You could not miss him because he was shirtless and displaying his unmistakable belly. *So much for Ema's claim that Carlos didn't live with her and had no contact with him.* I later found out that they were renting this home to the tune of $3,000+ per month. All this occurring the same time their million-dollar home in Plantation Acres was going through foreclosure proceedings; and none of the authorities questioned how they paid their rent—knowing the Valencias had NO legal means of employment!!

BTW, the theft of Ruth Hipp occurred *after* we filed our grand theft charges against the Valencias. Her misfortune could have been prevented if Detective Tighe and the Plantation P.D. had done their jobs back in 2007. They were quick to abuse an innocent victim (me), but let the criminals walk (entire Valencia family).

CHAPTER 27

Malicious Prosecution

Thanks to Patricia Wallace—an ace of a lawyer who took my malicious prosecution case against the Valencias on a contingency basis—Patricio and Ema were exposed once again as the liars they are; via her deposition. Shady and overweight lawyer Luis Fernandez even dropped them as clients, and they settled out of court for $10,000 in October 2008. It is believed they paid the settlement with the credit card of Carlos' most recent ponzi victim, Ruth Hipp (mentioned earlier). Luis Fernandez refused to divulge how Carlos and Ema paid him for his lawyer services.

On June 5, 2008, Carlos Casa Valencia appeared in Federal court for his bankruptcy hearing. His welcome in South Florida ran dry, and Judge Olsen dismissed his Chapter 13 with prejudice. In his ruling Judge Olsen wrote, "Carlos Casa Valencia is nothing more than a thief who preyed upon hard working victims. His actions in respect of the movants were despicable." Judge Olsen also blasted his lawyer (Carlos A. Santos) for acting in bad faith. *BTW, Santos worked in the same building as Luis Fernandez, the attorney who formerly represented Carlos and family.*

On August 3, 2009, Patricia Wallace was successful in winning a "Final Default Judgment Against Carlos Casa Valencia" in the amount of $187,561.38 on my behalf. To date, I have yet to see a penny, and the chances of any recovery are slim—at best. Some day I envision Carlos sitting in a courtroom in handcuffs and shackles awaiting the justice he rightly deserves. That will be my final judgment and peace of mind!

CHAPTER 28

Woman Shot to Death in Police Parking Lot

On April 25, 2008, Olidia Day Kerr was murdered in the Plantation Police Department parking lot after she had been crying and screaming for her life to a dispatcher about a crazed gunman who was following her in another vehicle intending to kill her. This went on for twenty minutes. Ms. Kerr's car was rammed by this armed man right outside Plantation headquarters. He then exited his vehicle and shot her while still in her vehicle. She got out and was able to run, but was shot dead outside the entrance of the police station. The murderer committed suicide at that point. You can listen to the chilling 911 call via this link: http://abcnews. go.com/video/playerIndex?id=5825845.

To show the callousness and disregard of citizens by *certain* members of the Plantation Police Department, both Richard Vincent and Phil Toman claimed the police did a good job responding to this incident. Try to comprehend—Olidia is shot dead outside the door of the Plantation police station and they claim they did a good job! *Why don't you go ahead and tell the family what a great job they did?*

This incident took place during the core of my problems with the Plantation Police Department. I simply wanted to demonstrate how their officers blatantly offer nothing but excuses for the shoddy work that's performed. I also would like to apologize to the Plantation police officers who continue to honor and uphold their oath to serve and protect its citizens and put their lives on the line every day. No disrespect to them.

CHAPTER 29

Three Years Later . . .

Three years after my initial conversation with internal affairs officer
Richard Vincent—and after numerous e-mails—I spoke with him again on
11/2/2010 and asked him about their investigative report on the Valencias.
He acted as if I had never spoken to him before. However, he did mail me
forms to file a formal complaint against the five officers who I felt were
negligent and abusive in their treatment of me back in 2007:

1. Officer Joel Stevenson—Let his partner abuse me and did nothing about
   it. Cuffed my hands so tight it caused welts on both wrists. Also had
   his report signed by an officer who wasn't present at the scene.

2. Sgt. Richard Vincent—When I called to file an initial complaint against
   the officers, he refused to take my complaint and investigate same. He
   told me to drop it.

3. Lt. Bruce Finney—Called at 7AM and inquired as to why I wasn't being
   a nice guy about the incident.

4. The anonymous officer who Stevenson, Vincent, and Finney covered
   up for. He is the officer who told me, "You should know what pain is.
   You're a boxer."

5. Det. William Tighe—Was belligerent towards me because I complained
   to his captain that he was not doing anything in relation to our case.

I learned via FaceBook that the Valencia family relocated to
Tallahassee, Florida. William Tighe did not update me on the Valencia's

move to Tallahassee—which was not surprising since I have never received any updates from this charlatan. Ninety-nine percent of policemen are good and fulfill their oath, but not the five men I encountered in Plantation.

Chief Larry Massey resigned unexpectedly—and their newly appointed chief of police (W. Howard Harrison) sports a wide smile complimenting his bushy mustache on the Plantation P.D. wesite. On 12/16/10, Chief Harrison wrote a short letter in response to my complaint advising that "upon being briefed" by Captain Funderburk, he was satisfied with the way his men performed their duties. *(What? But Captain Funderburk previously advised me he had no knowledge of my incident!)* And that's the last I heard from Chief Harrison who—by the way—is the supervisor of Sgt. Vincent, per civilian staff.

It's all a vicious cycle as one covers for the other, but *NEVER!* give up your rights if someone ever tries to take them from you.

Chief Harrison *did* put me in touch with records systems coordinator Donna Jones Wehbe, who provided me with a report from the September 2007 incident. This is how I found out Joel Stevenson was the officer who cuffed me and covered up for the punk cop who abused me.

After numerous messages and e-mails to the chief of police and mayor of Plantation, I finally received a phone call in May 2011 from Captain Funderburk—who answered on behalf of the officers. While sympathetic, he refused to address most of the issues. He claimed Detective Tighe did not have to file a report; the voluminous photos I gave to Tighe were unaccounted for; and the officers who abused me just used *bad judgment*—nothing that requires an investigation.

To date, Plantation P.D. still refuses to issue me some of the reports that I requested. I've found that in a small town like Plantation, you are out of luck when dealing with city government unless you have the big bucks to retain a lawyer. If not for the diligence of Carmel Cafiero and Patricia Wallace, our grand theft charges would have been ignored by the Plantation Police Department.

CHAPTER 30

The Charitable Challenge

We are coming up on the tenth anniversary of the terror attacks on the Twin Towers and the Pentagon. I will never forget those who made the ultimate sacrifice that fateful morning. After the attacks, we did everything we could to raise money for the many widows and orphans of fire and police. I fought in two charity bouts. And now I want to issue a challenge—despite my breathing complications and severe hip & shoulder disabilities—to the five cowards at Plantation P.D. who abused me; namely, Joel Stevenson, Richard Vincent, Bruce Finney, William Tighe, and the punk officer they all covered for. There will be more charity bouts in New York for the police and fire department widows and orphans, and I want each of you as an opponent in the ring against me. I'm 59 and disabled, but I still like my chances against a coward who hides behind a badge and a gun. (Again, no disrespect to the Plantation officers who continue to honor and uphold their oath and put their lives on the line every day to protect its citizens.)

> "In the ring there are no timeouts, no teammates, and no places to hide."

CHAPTER 31

Brown Grass in Plantation

The mayor claims the grass is greener in Plantation, but I've found it to be the darkest shade of brown. If this could happen to me, it can happen to anyone. An abusive officer still has his badge and his gun, a wise-guy lieutenant still covers for his men, an internal affairs sergeant lumps himself in with the good cops (99.9%), and a slacker detective allows a family of crooks to get away and ply their trade in another city.

Thanks to this motley crew, I no longer give the police the benefit of the doubt. As with anything else in life—when it happens to you, you learn it's for real.

I've attached a few pictures of the Valencia family so you can identify their faces. If you live in Tallahassee and you happen to cross their path, please run the other way! But if you ever have the opportunity to meet up with "Mr. Carlos-Ponzi-Scam-Artist" himself, **please report him to the authorities.**

Left to right: Sharon Casa Valencia; Ema Paolazzi (aka Ema Casa Valencia); Carlos Casa Valencia; and Alejandro Casa Valencia.

Alejandro and Sharon Casa Valencia

Patricio Casa Valencia

Carlos Casa Valencia—If you see this man, please report him to the authorities!

Before moving to Plantation, the Valencias plied their trade at other locations in Florida—including Miami and City Isles. Both Ema and Carlos have scammed countless individuals and banks out of millions of dollars to support their lavish lifestyle. They should have been stopped cold in Plantation, but were left unhindered [while] I was harassed. In light of this, I will continue to follow up on the Valencias' move to Tallahassee.

My dad was a police officer in New York City in the fifties and sixties. My brothers John and Jim were also police officers in New York City in the seventies, eighties and nineties. As a New York City firefighter, we responded to many alarms—along with cops—and had a mutual respect and support for each other. I cannot understand the animosity these five officers were projecting toward a citizen (me) they had sworn to serve and protect. While I always gave police the benefit of the doubt in incidents of claimed abuse, I will now be more inquisitive after my treatment by the Plantation Police Department.

In light of what happened to me, I have begun Job No. 51—Investigative Journalist! It is not one I sought, but one I must accept.

CHAPTER 32

In Conclusion

Unless you are disabled, diseased or have one foot in the grave, there are jobs available for everyone—even in this economy. If the one you find doesn't pay enough, then look for another to boost your coffers while still working your day job. Whenever I see politicians and world leaders lecture the masses on spending and social justice, I chuckle because all of them are filthy rich. Our current president is a fantastic example of "Do as I say, but not as I do."

I don't want to be considered right wing and conservative—or left wing and liberal—so I'll add George W. Bush (Obama's predecessor) as my second example. Both men and their families are wealthy beyond comparison to average Americans; yet, they have the audacity to preach about living within our means and sharing the wealth. If either were true to their word, they would curb their personal extravagance and redistribute what they own.

When seeking employment, put on a suit or the best clothes you own and go in person to inquire about a position. Even if there are no openings, you might make such an impression as to create one. All employers like a go-getter and would rather see someone in the flesh who may help with the bottom line. We've all heard the promises from politicians—which more often than not turn out to be lies—so the employer can't get a feel for an individual by only reading a pumped up resume. Like the politician, he or she might be impressive on paper, but depressive in person. Think about it as if you were the employer. Someone who asserts himself and applies in the flesh has the edge.

If you can't get the perfect job with the wages you expect, be prepared to settle for something less and work your way up. Go into a different field, if need be, but don't depend on anyone else to provide for you. It is not honorable and breeds failure. The only entity who benefits is the government. They dole out taxpayer money—which doesn't belong to them—and buy your vote while relegating you to serfdom. Those in power like dependency—no matter how you frame it—because without such, you might be a success and out-earn them. If this weren't the case, our leaders would lay out a blueprint for you to achieve success. You will learn that none of them were on welfare and received food stamps. So the question remains—*Why won't they share their success?* The answer is simple—*They don't want the competition.* A sliced up pie is acceptable for the masses, but the rich toppings are reserved *only* for them.

Don't let anyone fool you while they are trying to impose their agenda on you. Every job you apply for, intend to be the best and strive for greater. Never be beholden or sell your soul to manipulators for fame and fortune. Earn it for yourself and challenge everything to verify the truth. You are better than the rest, but you have to prove it—*And who better to count on for success than you?* If I can be a success, anybody can!

22655518R00077

Printed in Great Britain
by Amazon